UNDERSTANDING POETRY

JAMES REEVES

Understanding Poetry

HEINEMANN

LONDON

Heinemann Educational Books Ltd
LONDON MELBOURNE TORONTO
SINGAPORE CAPE TOWN
AUCKLAND IBADAN
HONG KONG

Published by
Heinemann Educational Books Ltd
15–16 Queen Street, Mayfair, London W.1
Printed in Great Britain by
Butler & Tanner Ltd
Frome and London

Contents

Acknowledgements

The author and publishers wish to thank the following publishers, authors and agents for permission to reprint copyright material:

Jonathan Cape Ltd for an extract from *In the Country* by W. H. Davies; Chatto and Windus Ltd for an extract from *Arms and the Boy* by Wilfred Owen; Eyre & Spottiswoode Ltd for an extract from *Dead Boy* by John Crowe Ransom; Faber & Faber Ltd for *Tea at the Palaz of Hoon* from *Collected Poems* by Wallace Stevens; Rupert Hart-Davis Ltd for *Field-Glasses* by Andrew Young; Leonard Woolf and The Hogarth Press Ltd for an extract from *To the Lighthouse* by Virginia Woolf; Liveright Publishing Corporation for *North Labrador* from *Collected Poems* by Hart Crane; Macmillan & Co. Ltd and the Trustees of the Hardy Estate for extracts from *A Broken Appointment* and *Weathers*, and the complete poem *I Look into my Glass*, from *Collected Poems* by Thomas Hardy; Macmillan & Co. Ltd and Mrs Iris Wise for *A Glass of Beer* by James Stephens; Professor Charles Madge for an extract from *Blocking the Pass*; Laurence Pollinger Ltd and Jonathan Cape Ltd for an extract from *Death of the Hired Man* from *Collected Poems* by Robert Frost; Routledge & Kegan Paul Ltd for *The Embankment, Conversion* and *Autumn* by T. E. Hulme; The Society of Authors, as the literary representative of the Estate of the late A. E. Housman, and Jonathan Cape Ltd, for *On Wenlock Edge* and *Others, I am not the First* from *Collected Poems* by A. E. Housman; The Literary Trustees of Walter De la Mare and the Society of Authors for *The Railway Junction* by Walter De la Mare; A. P. Watt & Son and International Authors N.V. for extracts from *The Cool Web* and *The Legs* by Robert Graves (from *Collected Poems* 1959 published by Cassell & Co. Ltd).

CHAPTER I

POETRY AND YOU

Not long ago twenty people were asked the question, 'Do you read poetry?' They were adults ranging in age from twenty-one to nearly seventy, a cross-section of society including teachers, factory-workers, a doctor, a professional musician, three farm-hands, several clerks and shop assistants. Of these twenty people, questioned individually, one said she read poetry constantly, pre-ferring it to all other recreations. One said he read it fairly often, mainly contemporary poems in magazines and anthologies. Four said they occasionally read poetry: they picked up a book perhaps once a year. The remaining fourteen said they never read poetry. Most were not hostile, though two or three thought it was rub-bish and were strongly opposed to it. The rest had nothing against it; they just weren't interested.

So if my sample was a fair one, as I am sure it was, it seems that at least seventy per cent of the adult population have little or no use for poetry. Another twenty per cent can do without it. Only one in ten regards it as of real value. Of course my sample was too small for the enquiry to be considered scientific. Nor did I take the experiment any further and try to discover the quality of the poetry read by the two who enjoyed it, nor the various reasons why the seventy per cent had little use for it. But I did ask one further question: 'Did you once read poetry?' To this question all but three answered unhesitatingly, 'Yes'. It seems that nearly everyone reads *some* poetry at school, and few continue to read it afterwards. Is poetry just something you are taught at school and forget when you go out into the world?

In this book I want to try especially to reach two classes of reader: first, the man or woman who feels a vague general approval for poetry but has never actually read much or troubled to sort out his ideas about it; the person who has a few favourite poems and has never felt much desire to extend the list. Secondly,

I want to reach the man or woman who, though generally intelligent and alert, has no use for poetry because it seems to have nothing for him or her in particular; the person who is indifferent but not actively hostile; the person who may enjoy a symphony concert or an exhibition of paintings, but to whom the written word, in verse form, is a closed book.

Poetry has been going on as long as human speech; it has engaged the interest of large numbers of people for many centuries; it has tempted devoted men and women away from worldly success, and it has won the passionate concern of men and women of all kinds and in all countries.

Moreover, the love of poetry is seldom a mere craze. Once it has been acquired, it is rarely lost. It is true that some readers enjoy it at school and later lose their enjoyment. This is probably because they have been taught either too well or too badly. An enthusiastic teacher whom they happen to like may induce in them a merely ephemeral interest in poetry; a bad teacher may put them off it for years, perhaps for life. But a reader of some maturity who discovers an interest in poetry for himself will probably never lose it.

The love of poetry is an infection to which no one is permanently immune. But many potential readers have been inoculated against it by the conditions of modern life and education. Poetry is a matter of private enjoyment. There were times, before mass education, and before the invention of printing, when poetry was something of a mass medium. There are still places of primitive civilization where poetry, usually in the form of song, is a collective cultural interest. But in Europe and America today this has long since ceased to be so. Attempts have been made, and are still being made, through the radio and other means, to revive the enjoyment of poetry as a collective activity. They haven't yet met with widespread success, so that it would be useless for me to discuss them. When I speak of 'poetry and you', I mean you personally, as a private individual. Now there is something of a reaction against the cultivation of the individual. We are more and more at the mercy of the mass media, more and more tempted to do things as members of this or that group. Poetry is badly adapted to group appreciation. We can enjoy music in a concert hall and pictures in an art gallery. We can admire feats of architecture and engineering in public, surrounded by our fellow-men. I don't want to underrate the work of those who organize public poetry readings, but these are still only a small contribution compared with the enjoyment of poetry in private.

It might be thought that the invention of printing, which meant the virtual extinction of the minstrel class and the group enjoyment of poetry in the halls of great nobles, might mean the end of poetry. It didn't. It meant, however, that poetry became more inward-looking, more a matter for the study, the bedroom, the place of retirement. Things may be changing once more, but I cannot write of poetry now except as something for the recreation of *you* in private, or at most you in the company of one or two friends.

Another thing about poetry which has tended to lessen its appeal to intelligent people nowadays is that it is essentially national, though not nationalistic. Progressive people are drawn to what has international appeal, especially painting, sculpture and music. They read prose literature from any country, translated if necessary into their own language. This gives an air of internationalism to their cultural lives. Only poetry obstinately refuses to be translated. That it *is* translated, and published in translation, does not alter this fact. Nobody really enjoys translated poetry, except when the translator has such originality of mind that he re-creates the poem anew in his own language. Few translators have this gift. Translated modern poetry is more a tribute to the new internationalism than anything very interesting or significant in itself. For the most part, it proves the point I am making. Poetry is untranslatable.

Fortunately the English-speaking world is immense, and no one who has been brought up to speak and write English is debarred from a share in what is the greatest cultural inheritance the world has ever known—English poetry. Whenever I use this word, I mean poetry written in the English language, whether by an American, an Australian, an African, or any other English-speaking person.

The love of poetry is an affair of the heart. No one can talk you into falling in love, or talk you out of it, or persuade you to love poetry rather than anything else. Falling in love can occur suddenly, irrationally and when least expected. Falling in love with poetry, however, is different in some ways from falling in love with a person. You can fall out of love with a person for quite insufficient reasons. You may mistake infatuation for being in love. This is not likely to happen between you and poetry, unless your earliest acquaintance has been on the wrong lines. Moreover, between you and poetry there can be no such thing as unrequited passion. Poetry cannot refuse your advances, cannot refuse to give to you as much as you give to her. Poetry is incapable of coldness, coquetry or infidelity. The love of poetry must also be an affair of the head. A two-year-old may fall in love with nursery rhymes for their pretty sound, but unless there is *some* sense in them, something to appeal to his dawning intelligence, his love will not take root.

Poetry is an affair of the heart, and no writer can make you fall in love. The best he can do is to introduce you to poems of all kinds, tell you which he likes best, and leave it at that. But the best poetry is inclined to be shy, needs 'bringing out'; and, since we are concerned with an affair of the head as well as of the heart, a certain amount of talk and explanation will be necessary. The best part of the book—as some reviewer is bound to discover—is the quotations. If all else fails, at least pick out these, read them, say them aloud, enjoy them if you can for their own sake. If you can enjoy these, you can enjoy others. In these pages you will meet poetry. Don't expect it to help you to 'get on in life'. It won't. It is what will help you to enjoy life once you have got on, or when you don't get on, or when you are sick of the whole business of getting on.

CHAPTER 2

THE TREE OF MAN

I have promised two things: poems and explanation. I shall talk about a good many poems. But one thing must be remembered: poetry can never be fully explained. It can be *felt*, and it can be talked about with profit. But there is no use whatever in talking about it if you don't feel it. I want to explain as much as I can; but there is always a mystery about poetry. If there were not, it would lose its fascination.

Let us look at a poem; then I will try to tell you what it means to me. I can't explain it, and I can't make you like it. I can only ask you to read it. My comments may perhaps illuminate the mystery of this poem, but they can't *explain* it. If the mystery is completely explained, in the sense of being explained away, it is no real mystery, and the poem is a failure. But I think that, however much you read it and however much I talk about it, its mystery will still exist unspoilt and unexplained. You may know this poem already. If so, have you ever read it searchingly? It is called *On Wenlock Edge* and it is by A. E. Housman.

> On Wenlock Edge the wood's in trouble;
> His forest fleece the Wrekin heaves;
> The gale, it plies the saplings double,
> And thick on Severn snow the leaves.
>
> 'Twould blow like this through holt and hanger
> When Uricon the city stood:
> 'Tis the old wind in the old anger,
> But then it threshed another wood.
>
> Then, 'twas before my time, the Roman
> At yonder heaving hill would stare:
> The blood that warmed an English yeoman,
> The thoughts that hurt him, they were there.

There, like the wind through woods in riot,
Through him the gale of life blew high;
The tree of man was never quiet:
Then 'twas the Roman, now 'tis I.

The gale, it plies the saplings double,
It blows so hard, 'twill soon be gone.
Today the Roman and his trouble
Are ashes under Uricon.

This is an expression of personal feeling. The poet is under the influence of some deep trouble, and the pressure of his emotion impels him to an outburst of feeling. But his mood is under strict control. He does not burst out in wild denunciation of fate or human misery. The verse form is simple and regular, the rhythm measured and slow. So much for the general impression conveyed by the form of the poem.

There is a certain dramatic element in Housman's handling of his subject. It is as if he wants to stand away from himself in order to project his state of mind more effectively. He puts a distance between himself and his emotions—a distance not of place but of time. In the first stanza[1] he sketches, in four clear firm lines, the picture of a Shropshire wood torn by the gales of Autumn. Next he takes a jump back two thousand years and imagines the same scene in Roman times. There was then a fortress town, Uriconium, manned by Roman legionaries. The wind at that time would blow just as fiercely, but the wood was not the same; it would have died or been cut down and replaced by another. In contrast, however, to the trees, the Roman who stared at them is connected by human ties and the human condition to the Englishman who now stares at them in his turn.

The blood that warms an English yeoman,
The thoughts that hurt him, they were there.

This gives the poet a feeling of kinship with the Roman soldier, whose troubles he can share in retrospect. The Roman was troubled by the same feelings and passions as now make the

[1] I shall use the word 'stanza' throughout, in preference to the more usual 'verse', to denote the groups of lines of which a poem is composed. 'Verse' is used in another sense, and it is necessary to avoid confusion.

Englishman suffer. But the final thought that once more chills the mind of the poet is that, while he (the poet) still lives and suffers, the man whose trouble he shares is dead. In this way, he implies, while to some extent we can share the troubles of all humanity, and gain comfort from the thought that 'the tree of man was never quiet', yet we are cut off from the dead by the very fact that we are still alive to suffer.

There is much more to be said about this poem, especially about its language and versification; but let us not stop to consider that now. The main point about *On Wenlock Edge* is that it is about the universality of suffering, and the comfort that is to be drawn from contemplating the human condition and not concentrating each on our own suffering in isolation. This is the main meaning of the experience to Housman. Does it mean exactly the same to the reader?

The poem cannot mean to us quite what it meant to Housman. We are not told exactly what his trouble was, and obviously he would have been obsessed by it in a way we cannot be. Otherwise he could not have written with passion. But he is not trying to dwell on it, he is trying to escape from it, to see it in terms of the human condition as it is at all times. He seeks relief in the thought that some Roman soldier stood once on the same spot and cursed his lot; but even while his suffering is relieved, he is partly cheated of relief by the thought that the Roman is dead and no longer suffering. Each of us must bear his troubles alone. None the less, there is also the added relief, sardonically expressed, that comes from the unspoken thought: the Roman and his trouble are dead. Before long I too will be dead and my trouble with me. We are left in some doubt as to what the final mood is—one of deep despair or one of final reconciliation. Both of these possibilities are there. More than one element combines to make up the mood of the poem. Comfort and despair are present together, as so often in our own moods. There is no final resolution.

Just as Housman gained comfort from the thought that he shared his distress with the unknown Roman soldier, and that he was not the first, nor would be the last, to suffer, so we are indebted to Housman for the revelation he gives us of the nature of our own malaise. Although the poem is, in one sense, profoundly pessimistic (a word often used in describing Housman), the total effect is not depressing: we gain from it a renewal of the knowledge that we do not suffer alone; Housman opens for us windows into space and time, through which we can gain a vision of things beyond our own immediate condition. It is introspective brooding upon our condition in isolation which is depressing. We are given a glimpse of Housman's Shropshire as a distant and very beautiful setting for his distress; and from modern times we are taken back two thousand years to Roman Britain. In this way our own obsessive suffering is universalized and made more bearable —because more comprehensible.

Whether or not it is true that 'the tree of man was never quiet', we cannot be certain. What is certain is that this restlessness of spirit manifests itself wherever human beings are to be found. Armies of healers and reformers are at work to increase happiness and restore the psyche to its primal innocence, its lost joy; but until their work is finished, an event of which there is no immediate sign, we shall need relief from the outer pressures and inner conflicts which trouble us. Matthew Arnold believed in a great future for poetry as the healer and restorer of the spirit. There are few signs that any significant number of people have as yet found it to be so. But poetry always has this potentiality, if we care to discover it.

We cannot speak with certainty of the future of poetry, any more than we can be certain that the human condition will always be a troubled one. But just as we know that, till now, distress has always existed, so we know that poetry has existed from the earliest times as a manifestation of the human spirit and a relief from, or expression of, emotion. The forms of poetry have changed, and its uses and purposes have varied from age to age. One thing is certain: the primary purpose of poetry is magical. This is evidenced by what we know of primitive peoples still living in remote parts of the world in the conditions which have prevailed for hundreds of years. Magical rituals, especially those connected with the primary facts of birth, survival and death, are accompanied by words in the shape of magical formulas. They are also often accompanied by music and dancing. The words supply an indispensable intellectual element in what is largely a physical activity. Such activity was mainly on a group basis. When a community is occupied with its own survival, all its ritual is connected with group emotions and group needs. There would be no place for a poem such as *On Wenlock Edge*. This poem is an indication of how far western man has travelled on the road from primitive collectivism to sophisticated individualism. When a people is concerned with survival, it has no time for the cultivation of private feeling. Most of the chants of primitive people are traditional, though the stock may be enriched by frequent additions. They are stored up in the collective memory and never written down, except by scholars and anthropologists. In our own midst we still have communities of school children who possess and hand down a body of folklore of much the same kind, some of it sung, some spoken, all connected magically with play and other concerns of child life.

I have said that poems, even as a part of primitive ritual, supply the intellectual element in what is principally a physical activity. It may not be thought that there is anything very intellectual about the folk rhymes of children and primitive people. But as a word is never simply a noise—even the earliest cries of infants have meaning—it is something intellectual. You can make a dog 'understand' the words 'Lie down' by sheer repetition; you can train it to obey certain spoken commands by a process of conditioning. Dogs are very amenable to such conditioning up to a certain point. We rightly think of them as 'almost human'. But a child will surpass a dog in understanding in a very short time indeed, and the fully mature dog will seem very stupid in comparison with a mere infant.

In the human species the understanding and use of language is an essential part of growing up. From the very first, speech sounds, and later words, are essentially magical to a child. We are so used to employing words for merely material and physical ends that we forget their magical origin. Our lives are cluttered up with written information of a purely utilitarian character, so that, in our materialistic civilization, we tend to think of the language of parliamentary acts and commercial documents as the primary function of language, and its more magical uses as unimportant, trivial or frivolous. It is not so with children. To an infant each new word it learns has magical properties, giving it power over the objects it learns to name. That is why its first words are those denoting its parents. The first need is the need for security; as soon as a child learns that it can gain the attention of a parent by uttering a special sound, that sound acquires magical properties. Doubtless an infant needs to gain power over its parents for material ends; but in the infant mind there is no division between the material and the spiritual or emotional. The need for physical survival is inseparable from the need for emotional security. Moreover, the sounds which an infant makes to express pleasure are also of magical origin and significance. The sound made by an infant on seeing a flower or a toy, or moving water, or leaves in the sunlight, is a poetic utterance arising from the need to communicate pleasure. The most primitive poem, far more primitive than the tribal rain chant, which by comparison is sophisticated—the most primitive poem is an infant's cry of pleasure.

The desire to communicate, to express, to give voice to emotion, is the root from which all poetry springs. All poetry has to do with communication; but it is not merely *saying* something in a special way, although many poets have written in this belief. It is a special form of words which has the power, magical power, to evoke certain responses in the hearer or reader, and this power never leaves it. There have been many attempts to write poems on some other basis than this, and we shall discuss them later. But the reason why poetry has virtue at all times lies in the need of man for magical formulations, word-patterns, which give expression to emotional or intellectual situations perpetually recurrent in the human condition.

It would take too long to discuss the importance of language to man. Indeed it is so self-evident that we are inclined to forget it. But man is above all, and has always been, a speaking animal. Whatever aspects of his life are purely physical, he cannot live for long on a purely physical plane. As soon as language enters, he is an intellectual being. The difference between the word 'table' and the thing 'table' is something a dog can grasp—if only dimly. But the gap is immense, and as soon as we learn to use words with more than a purely material significance—'hunger', for instance, or 'love' or 'music'—we are outside the plane of animal understanding and on a largely intellectual one. The gap between even the most obscenely physical word and the thing or act it denotes is immense. Poetry, therefore, which is composed of words, is necessarily an intellectual manifestation of the human spirit; and unless we so far debase intellect as to become sub-human, there will be a need and a place for poetry. How then, you may ask, can seventy per cent or more of civilized English-speaking people get along without poetry? Briefly, they don't: they use substitutes. I will have more to say about this later.

I will end this chapter by referring once more to what I regard as true poetry. For it is unhealthy to live for long on substitutes, and one purpose of this book is to help you to choose the real and avoid substitutes. We began by listening to the voice of a modern English poet expressing a sense of community with those long dead. We might end by taking the words of a poet of Roman times whose work might have been read by Housman's dead soldier. But that would mean reading a foreign language, and I prefer to keep to English. Moreover, the English poetry of that day, if any had survived, would be no more comprehensible to us. To find something in more or less the same language as Housman used we must jump a thousand years or so from Roman times. Here is a stanza in which can be heard some stirring of the wind that blew through the tree of man in medieval times.

> Western wind, when will thou blow,
> The small rain down can rain?
> Christ, if my love were in my arms
> And I in my bed again!

No one knows how long ago this stanza was made up; probably it was part of a long lost traditional ballad which happened to take the fancy of some studious monk, who thereupon transcribed these few lines, together with its tune, in the fourteenth century manuscript now preserved in the British Museum. Whatever its origins, the stanza expresses clearly and directly one heartfelt utterance of the human spirit as it breathes through the restless tree of man. Only when lovers suffer no longer the anguish of each other's absence will poetry such as this cease to have value. No one can fully explain the significance of these lines; a modern reader, unless he is peculiarly insensitive or over-sophisticated, can only feel its magic and acknowledge its power to touch and disturb his thoughts.

CHAPTER 3

POETRY AND ITS SUBSTITUTES

In England, during the reign of Queen Elizabeth, two kinds of poetry existed side by side—folk poetry and aristocratic poetry. Folk poetry was mostly connected with popular music and was a form of song. It had existed for many centuries, and still exists as folk song, but only in the remoter parts of the British Isles, where modern urban civilization has been slow to penetrate. In America, too, genuine folk song is still to be found in the remoter regions, in a more vigorous state than in Britain.

But most of what we now think of as poetry—the kind of which Housman's *On Wenlock Edge*, discussed in the last chapter, is an example—has developed from the aristocratic tradition.

After the introduction of printing towards the end of the fifteenth century it became fashionable among educated men and women to write and read poetry. This practice did not spread quickly, but by the end of Elizabeth's reign it was firmly established. Collections of poems by various writers became widely known and read among the aristocracy. The most famous of these was Tottel's Miscellany (1557), which contained, among many others, poems by the two Tudor nobles, Sir Thomas Wyatt and the Earl of Surrey. Almost every young nobleman who wished to be considered a complete gentleman was able to turn out a sonnet in praise of his mistress or a verse compliment to an aristocrat whom he wished to flatter. Even kings and queens, among them Henry VIII and Elizabeth, composed words to be set to music. The writing and reading of poems was as much a part of the normal equipment of a lady or gentleman as going to horse-races is now.

Not all the poetry written at this time was good. Much of it was pedestrian and commonplace, but technically it was of a fair average standard, and at its best, in the final decade of the sixteenth century, it rose to great lyric heights in the songs of the lutenists and dramatists and the sonnets of Shakespeare.

Why, you may wonder, was this outburst of poetry aristocratic? The reason is simply that only the wealthy had the leisure and means to be educated. It was also the nobility who patronized the poets. Until the development of trade at the end of the century wealth was concentrated in the hands of the landed class, and this class was the titled aristocracy. By the end of the century the exclusively aristocratic character of the educated class had given place to something broader, largely owing to the growth of grammar schools for the education of poor men's sons. Many of the dramatists at the end of the century, Shakespeare included, had sprung from the merchant classes. Now it is the virtue of the English aristocratic tradition that it was always able to strengthen and renew itself by drawing in members of the other classes. So that the literary tradition in England, as distinct from the popular tradition, remained essentially aristocratic. Shakespeare, the son of a country tradesman, was enabled by his talents to obtain the patronage and favour of noblemen and ultimately to become a landed gentleman himself.

His work sprang partly from popular drama, partly from aristocratic poetry. This was its strength. It became national in character and appeal. With the broadening of social opportunity in the seventeenth century, and in particular the advantages gained by the trading classes after the Civil War, poetry lost its exclusively aristocratic quality, but the poems themselves retained the old spirit. It is not possible to notice a distinctively middle-class kind of poetry in the seventeenth century, even though it was written by men who were not of the aristocracy. That came later. The poems of the nobleman Sir Thomas Wyatt, written during the reign of Henry VIII, were lyrics of personal feeling which derived something of their quality from his Italian models. Poems written a century and more later, though no longer aristocratic in origin, still bore the stamp of Wyatt's lyricism. Many other kinds of poetry were written in England and America between the beginning of the reign of Queen Elizabeth and the end of the reign of Queen Victoria, but the tradition of personal lyricism first planted by Wyatt persisted and has not yet died out. Even in the poems of Walt Whitman, the first consciously democratic poet, the note of personal lyricism can be heard. True, Whitman sometimes claimed to be the voice of America, but it is not only for his somewhat noisy declaration of national feeling that he is read today. Some readers prefer his quieter, more personal poems.

The point I have been making is that poetry, as I write of it here, is traditionally connected with the cultivation of the individual. In the days of Sir Thomas Wyatt and the Earl of Surrey only the landed aristocracy had time to cultivate their private sensibilities. Even Chaucer, marvellous as is his achievement in the fourteenth century, lacks the note of intimate revelation we hear in Wyatt, and speaks more for the court which was his patron. In order to underline my meaning, let us stop and read one of Wyatt's poems:

> There was never nothing more me pained,
> Nor nothing more me moved,
> As when my sweetheart her complained
> That ever she me loved.
> Alas the while!

> With piteous look she said and sighed:
> 'Alas, what aileth me
> To love and set my wealth so light
> On him that loveth not me?
> Alas the while!

> 'Was I not well void of all pain
> When that nothing me grieved?
> And now with sorrows I must complain,
> And cannot be relieved.
> Alas the while!

> 'My restful nights and joyful days
> Since I began to love
> Be take from me; all thing decays,
> Yet can I not remove.
> Alas the while!'

> She wept and wrung her hands withal,
> The tears fell in my neck;
> She turned her face and let it fall;
> Scarcely therewith could speak.
> Alas the while!

> Her pains tormented me so sore
> That comfort had I none,
> But cursed my fortune more and more
> To see her sob and groan:
> Alas the while!

Here is a poem written, like others throughout the centuries that succeeded, in the belief that the intimate concerns of a man and woman in love are fit matter for poetry. This is not, of course, the only subject, but it has proved one of the most persistently interesting to poets through the ages.

I am not writing a history of poetry, but it is necessary, in order to discuss what poetry is, to know something of what it was. There is nothing particularly sixteenth century about Wyatt except his language. His feeling is 'modern'—in other words, human. Now anyone who maintains that we can do without poetry is really saying that we can do without the cultivation of personal emotion. If this is so, it seems to me that we face the prospect of an immense impoverishment of life. We all have as much time now as an Elizabethan nobleman had in the sixteenth century for the cultivation of personal feeling and the enrichment of our individuality. This individuality is unique, and if we sacrifice it to an ideal of the collective State we are pursuing the ideal of an ant civilization. Wherever there are fully articulate human beings, living their lives to the full, there is poetry, which is indissolubly connected with the refinement of personality. To put it more crudely, if you believe you are a man or woman, if you believe in 'the pursuit of happiness' and that happiness means personal happiness, not some mindless animal contentment, some insect acquiescence in mechanical routine, you believe in the ideals of poetry. Still, in saying that the seventy per cent who do without poetry are, as I am convinced they are, the poorer for it, let us be reasonable. They have a good many things Sir Thomas Wyatt didn't have: the radio, the cinema, the popular magazine, the daily press, television. Undoubtedly, thousands of viewers of the television screen are beguiled for hours by alluring advertisements of commercial products. Are not the advertisement pages of the glossy magazines full of clever and fascinating ideas? Moreover, much advertising copy is composed with real skill and a feeling for language. One of the truest and best poets of our time, the Scottish-born Norman Cameron, wrote advertising copy for a living. I would be the first to admit that the sort of mental fare which a good advertising copy-writer offers has considerable appeal.

As you voyage to Rhodes and Crete, to Alexandria and Haifa, to Peloponnesus and Piraeus, you follow the routes of the Phoenician traders and Egyptian barges. You sail the waters across which Paris spirited Helen of Troy. The Seven Wonders of the pagan world are at every point of the compass that guide you through the mild and myth-misted Mediterranean.

Tiny sailing ships trap the sun in their brilliant sails as they bob and dip in your wake. The mountains of the gods loom over you as you drop anchor under the majestic shadow of Olympus, which you may first spy over a convivial glass, or through the saloon window over a crisp salad or hearty roast. Odysseus, the Golden Fleece, the Parthenon, the romantic shores of Yugoslavia, the Bosphorus and Albania, the hallowed hills of Galilee, the breath-taking Pyramids and the inscrutable Sphinx, the labyrinth at Cnossos . . . were there ever so many successive wonders as on these superb cruise calls?

How better can you escape from this workaday, humdrum world? Nobly you travel on . . . Did Helen really love Paris? Were handsome youths and lovely maidens truly sacrificed to the Minotaur? Did Unicorns exist? How memorable each day will be for you . . . Days of escape from the mundane world of dish-washing and office wrangles. You glide back in a cruising time-machine through aeons to the days of old, when gods were bold and crusaders had their day.

This can be guaranteed to stir a sluggish imagination, to arouse the spirit of restlessness and discovery; it slips smoothly off the tongue and seductively into the ear. It breathes romance. Clever people are apt to sneer at it, but this is not helpful. For there are hundreds of thousands who are taken in by it; who wallow in it when they would not open a book of the most perfect poems ever written; whose imagination can feed upon it with apparent satisfaction. Instead of dismissing it with a sneer, I prefer to give the devil his due and admit that it is a sort of poetry: substitute poetry. An appetite gorged on substitutes becomes in the end jaded. That is what is the matter with fake poetry of this kind. The difference between effective advertising copy and even average poetry is that the former is based on the unworthy motive of trying to sell you something you don't want. It aims at trying to make a fortune for someone who doesn't deserve it. It cost the writer and his employer nothing in emotional experience; worst of all, it is parasitic on true literature. Without original poetry to suck its life from, it would wither and die. The enemy is not the obviously bad; it is the substitute that looks like the real thing, so that only the expert can tell the difference.

But advertising copy is a comparatively crude substitute for poetry. There are many who would indignantly protest that they can easily tell the difference, and still they have no use for real poetry. What about the 'lyrics' for popular songs and musical comedies? Well, these too are a sort of poetry, at their best clever and well-turned; at their worst, clumsy, imitative and soon lost in the tide that streams from Tin Pan Alley. Still, the best popular songs have lasted a good many years and, at least for our time, passed into folk memory. They are popular art, not to be wholly dismissed, but not possessing the power to satisfy which true poetry has.

Then there is the short story and the novel. Why read poetry when you can entirely forget yourself in J. D. Salinger's touching story of an adolescent, *The Catcher in the Rye?* No one who reads this, or the novels of William Faulkner, Graham Greene or Carson McCullers could be called illiterate or indifferent to the written word. Indeed, in some of these there is something of the poet, just as in poets such as Chaucer, Spenser, Browning and Frost there was something of the novelist, or at least of the short-story writer. It would be a long and not too fruitful job to discuss the relations between poetry and fiction. But everybody admits the merits of fiction; they need no demonstration. What we have to talk about is the purpose and nature of poetry. Has poetry got anything which fiction has not? Here is a paragraph from a famous novel, *To the Lighthouse* by the modern English novelist, Virginia Woolf,

The house was left; the house was deserted. It was left like a shell on a sandhill to fill with dry salt grains now that life had left it. The long night seemed to have set in; the trifling airs, nibbling, the clammy breaths, fumbling, seemed to have triumphed. The saucepan had rusted and the mat decayed. Toads had nosed their way in. Idly, aimlessly, the swaying shawl swung to and fro. A thistle thrust itself between the tiles in the larder. Swallows nested in the drawing-room; the floor was strewn with straw; the plaster fell in shovelfuls; rafters were laid bare; rats carried off this and that to gnaw behind the wainscots. Tortoise-shell butterflies burst from the chrysalis and pattered their life out on the window pane.

What has poetry got, you may ask, that this hasn't? This is no advertising copy, crudely appealing to the tired imagination. It is real imaginative writing, personally felt and observed, evocative yet concrete. In all but outward form it is a poem. Some may say, 'Of course it isn't a poem; it doesn't rhyme and it has no metre.' But that objection, I am afraid, won't do. The majority of poems are in some sort of regular, rhymed verse, it is true. But verse isn't in itself poetry. We shall come to that. Meanwhile, read this:

Full of life now, compact, visible, I, forty years old the eighty-third year of the States, to one a century hence or any number of centuries hence, to you yet unborn these, seeking you. When you read these I that was visible am become invisible, now it is you, compact, visible, realizing my poems, seeking me, fancying how happy you were if I could be with you and become your comrade; be it as if I were with you. (Be not too certain but I am now with you.)

This is not, on the face of it, very different in form from the prose passage I quoted just now from Virginia Woolf. As a matter of fact, it is a complete poem by Walt Whitman. I have printed it as prose, just to fool you. Here is how it appears in Whitman's *Leaves of Grass*:

Full of life now, compact, visible,
I, forty years old the eighty-third year of the States,
To one a century hence or any number of centuries hence,
To you yet unborn these, seeking you.
When you read these I that was visible am become invisible,
Now it is you, compact, visible, realizing my poems, seeking me,
Fancying how happy you were if I could be with you and become your
    comrade;
Be it as if I were with you. (Be not too certain but I am now with you.)

You must honestly admit that the way it is printed, in un-rhymed lines of varying length, doesn't appear to make all that difference. Yet there is a world of difference.

The Virginia Woolf passage *is* a sort of poem which has found its way into a novel. It is a lyrical interlude whose artistic just-ification is that it bridges a gap of years between the action that goes before and the action that comes after it. Now a good deal of poetry, good and bad, has found its way into the prose writings of our time, especially fiction, but also biography and books of travel. This is, if you like, a sort of diluted poetry; not a substitute but a derivative, as a scientist might say. Paragraphs of poetic prose are liable to crop up anywhere. It is a matter of opinion whether this makes for better prose or not. What is certain is that it won't do as a complete substitute for poetry. In Chaucer's time there was no prose fiction, so story-tellers had to get their prose into verse. In our time poetry has become so rare and unsaleable that poetic writing gets into prose works. My own opinion is that the two are better kept apart.

The poem I quoted above, first as prose and then as free verse, is quite different in character and intention from the passage by Virginia Woolf. It is a total statement of an imaginative experience, an affirmation of personal belief. On the surface it actually looks less poetical than the Virginia Woolf passage. It is none the less a poem. It has unique value, detached from everything else Whitman or any other poet wrote. Its value resides in itself. True, Whitman's work is of increased importance seen as a whole. None the less, every part of it is a unique contribution to the poetry of its time and all time.

To sum up, then, what has been said in this chapter. That most people live without reading poetry doesn't prove there is no place for it. On the contrary, the need for poetry of some sort is shown by the demand for substitutes in the form of popular reading matter and popular songs. Moreover, there is a good deal of con-cealed poetry mixed up in novels and other prose writing. What we have to do, therefore, is to try to find out the essential diff-erences between poetry and prose, and so discover the real nature of poetry.

CHAPTER 4

WHAT IS POETRY?

We now come to the question, What is poetry? I may as well say at the start that this is going to be a difficult chapter to write. But we can't discuss poetry for long without attempting some sort of definition. Nobody talks about man's other artistic activities, such as architecture, or sculpture, or painting, or music, without a clear idea of what he is talking about. Most people would agree to call music the organization of sounds into a meaningful arrangement, or some such definition; painting is the creation of meaningful arrangements of line and colour. Experts on music and painting might disagree as to what exactly constitutes 'meaning', but they would not disagree much about the nature of these two arts. Yet people have disagreed radically and even passionately as to what poetry is. Most experts would agree to call certain literary works poems; but when it comes to agreeing on a definition of poetry that would cover all such works, there the trouble begins.

Why not try to define poetry in the same way as we define music or painting? Suppose we call poetry the creation of meaningful arrangements of words. But this won't do. It covers almost everything we can do with words. Even as I write down these sentences, I am creating meaningful arrangements of words. But this is not poetry. Everyone can see that. As a matter of fact, what I am writing, as you almost certainly know already, is prose: if you want to be more precise, you can call it expository prose, as distinct from, say, narrative or descriptive prose. It is the prose of reasoned argument.

By comparison, let us look at a few lines of poetry which most people are familiar with.

> The boast of heraldry, the pomp of power,
> And all that beauty, all that wealth e'er gave,
> Await alike th'inevitable hour:
> The paths of glory lead but to the grave.

This is a stanza from Gray's *Elegy written in a Country Church-yard*, which everyone will agree is poetry. Then you may say that poetry is words arranged in a regular pattern of rhymed and accented lines. Apart from the fact that we have already seen how a poem may be unrhymed and irregular in form, this simply won't do as a definition. What about this? Would you call it poetry?

> In England once there reigned a king,
>   A tyrant fierce and fell,
> Who for to gain himself a crown,
>   Gave sure his soul to Hell:
> Third Richard was this tyrant's name,
>   The worst of all the three;
> That wrought such deeds of deadly dole,
>   That worser could not be.
>
> For his desires were still (by blood)
>   To be made England's king,
> Which he to gain that golden prize,
>   Did many a wondrous thing:
> He slaughtered up our noble peers,
>   And chiefest in this land,
> With every one that likely was
>   His title to withstand.

Few, I think, would call this poetry. It is altogether too flat, forced and mechanical. It is nothing but a piece of prose narrative chopped up into regular lines and made to rhyme. It has nothing in common with the stanza from Gray's *Elegy* except the possession of regular rhythm and rhyme. We can all agree to call both examples verse, and it is verse, not poetry, which is the true opposite of prose. Yet many do not realize this. They speak of poetry as if it were simply verse. They think that if you take a story and tell it in verse, you are saying it in poetry. This is not true.

There are also people who deny that poetry can be defined at all. They prefer to call it simply 'verse' and leave it at that. But if poetry were merely verse, it would not be worthy of the attention it has attracted during all the centuries of its existence. Nor would there be any foundation for our feeling that the lines from Gray's *Elegy* are something quite different from the lines about Richard the Third. As a matter of fact, the latter is the beginning of a ballad entitled *The Life and Death of King Richard the Third*. It was probably composed in the time of Queen Elizabeth. If it is all on this flat and uninspired level, you may say, what on earth was the purpose of telling such a story in verse? Would it not have been just as good, or better, in prose? The answer to this question is historical, and it is worth noting. At the time of Elizabeth there were many thousands of people who could not read and had no books. Yet they liked stories, and they liked singing songs a lot more than English people do now. It was customary, therefore, for story-tellers to make up their stories in verse form, so that people could remember them and repeat them to others. Such stories were often printed on ballad-sheets or broadsides, as they were called, and sold at fairs or markets. Among any group of friends there would usually be at least one who could read, and this reader would possess a store of ballad-sheets to read or sing to others. People who cannot read often have astonishing memories, so that, once the verse story had been read or sung a number of times, many people in the group would know it by heart. They had a considerable appetite for new tales, and did not much care about the quality of the verse in which they were told, except that it must be regular enough in form to be easily learnt by heart. For this is the purpose of verse: to make interesting happenings, whether true or imaginary, easily memorable. Everyone knows the rhyme composed long ago by an anonymous author to make it easy for us to remember the length of the months: 'Thirty days hath September'. So poetry has been defined by one writer as 'memorable speech'; but this is the definition of verse, not poetry. For when verse is composed for people who can read, the mere memorability is not important. Many people do in fact learn poems by heart, even when they can read; but this is for the pleasure they gain, not because they would forget them otherwise.

We have seen, then, that there are two main divisions in the art or craft of writing: prose and verse. We have seen too that poetry is not simply verse. It is not always easy to recognize the difference, and experts might disagree in some cases as to whether a particular passage was poetry or just verse. So we have next to discuss the difference between poetry and verse. In this way we shall get nearer to a definition of poetry. Let us start by glancing at an example of prose. Here is the opening of Emily Brontë's novel, *Wuthering Heights*.

1801—I have just returned from a visit to my landlord—the solitary neighbour that I shall be troubled with. This is certainly a beautiful country! In all England I do not believe that I could have fixed on a situation so completely removed from the stir of society. A perfect misanthropist's Heaven: and Mr Heathcliff and I are such a suitable pair to divide the desolation between us. A capital fellow! He little imagined how my heart warmed towards him when I beheld his black eyes withdraw so suspiciously under their brows, as I rode up, and when his fingers sheltered themselves with a jealous resolution, still further in his waistcoat as I announced my name.

This, you will agree, is a plain prose statement. The writer is introducing her narrative, and she has a long and involved story to tell. It will contain descriptive passages of great beauty, and conversational passages of great power and pathos. It will narrate harrowing and exciting experiences, and it will leave the final impression of a great tragic drama. Emily Brontë also wrote poems, and she might have attempted to unfold her tremendous story in verse. It is well she did not. She had not the power to do so, and there was no poetic form, outside perhaps Shakespearean tragedy, large enough, flexible enough and capable of sufficient subtlety and variation to express everything she put into her prose novel. She uses prose for a variety of purposes: to describe the scene, to narrate the events, and above all, to record the speech, the feelings and the thoughts of her characters in as faithful a manner as possible, so as to make the story credible and convincing.

Let us turn now to the opening of another dramatic story, this time a poem of great length and power, Coleridge's *Rime of the Ancient Mariner*.

It is an ancient Mariner,
And he stoppeth one of three.

'By thy long grey beard and glittering eye,
Now wherefore stopp'st thou me?

'The Bridegroom's doors are open'd wide,
And I am next of kin;
The guests are met, the feast is set:
May'st hear the merry din.'

He holds him with his skinny hand,
'There was a ship,' quoth he.
'Hold off! unhand me, grey-beard loon!'
Eftsoons his hand dropt he.

He holds him with his glittering eye—
The Wedding Guest stood still,
And listens like a three years' child:
The Mariner hath his will.

It will be seen at once that Coleridge is using a quite different
medium from Emily Brontë and also from the anonymous author
of *The Life and Death of King Richard the Third*. He is using the
resources of language in a much more compressed and compelling
way. The two speakers are not presented realistically; they are,
as it were, flashed upon our consciousness as two performers in an
action of great dramatic significance. Only three characteristics
of the Mariner are noted: his long grey beard, his glittering eye,
and his skinny hand. The first indicates his great age and his
appearance as a sort of prophetic figure; the second suggests an
obsession amounting almost to madness; the skinny hand is
enough to suggest the emaciated condition of one who has been
through a severe physical trial. It is hinted that the Mariner is an
object of awe. Everything in these stanzas implies that we are
present at the opening of a tale of immense significance; the
atmosphere is tense with the coming drama and heavy with the
threat of terrible events. The abruptness, the swiftness and
the economy of writing tell us that the author is possessed by
the terrific import of what he has begun to tell: there is no time for
the leisured discursiveness of prose. The events may be as terrible
and as harrowing as those in *Wuthering Heights*, but they will
be handled in an entirely different way.

The peculiar strength of Coleridge's opening stanzas derives from two sources: the compression of the language, suggesting hidden power; and the strongly pictorial and acoustic[1] qualities, especially the swift march of the rhythm.

Coleridge has used the outward form of the old ballads, but he has made it entirely his own. The flat, uninspired jog-trot of some of the old ballad tales has quite disappeared, and a new, absolutely personal element has been introduced. This is what I think we can only call the magical element. If magic is a hidden power, springing we do not know whence, then the quality that distinguished *The Ancient Mariner* from mere verse must be called magic. If verse is memorable speech, then *The Ancient Mariner* is magical speech. Its words are full of suggestion, of unrevealed meaning, a meaning which will grow out of them under the influence of the reader's thought and imagination, as the oak grows out of the acorn under the influence of sunlight and moisture. No one who thinks about an acorn with a completely fresh mind can fail to see that it is essentially magical, since magic implies the inevitable yet unexpected, the utterly unexplained. Who, seeing an acorn for the first time, could imagine an oak-tree growing out of it? And yet, through familiarity, the connection between the acorn and the oak becomes inevitable, though for ever unexplained. I believe that all true poetry contains some particle, however small, of this organic magic. Some writers have claimed that poems are made: I prefer to think of them as having grown.

We shall look at many different kinds of poem; but in order to grasp firmly this essential point, let us look at yet one more poem —this time a complete one, Keats' *La Belle Dame Sans Merci*— in which the magical element is predominant.

> 'O what can ail thee, knight-at-arms,
>   Alone and palely loitering?
> The sedge has withered from the lake,
>   And no birds sing.

---

[1] I use the word 'acoustic' simply to mean 'sound qualities'—rhythm, rhyme, arrangement of vowels and consonants. I might have used the more familiar word 'musical', but I want to avoid any possible confusion with music itself, a quite different thing from poetry.

'O what can ail thee, knight-at-arms,
    So haggard and so woe-begone?
The squirrel's granary is full,
    And the harvest's done.

'I see a lily on thy brow
    With anguish moist and fever dew,
And on thy cheeks a fading rose
    Fast withereth too.'

'I met a lady in the meads,
    Full beautiful—a faery's child:
Her hair was long, her foot was light,
    And her eyes were wild.

'I made a garland for her head,
    And bracelets too, and fragrant zone.
She looked at me as she did love,
    And made sweet moan.

'I set her on my pacing steed,
    And nothing else saw all day long,
For sidelong would she bend, and sing,
    A faery's song.

'She found me roots of relish sweet,
    And honey wild and manna dew;
And sure in language strange she said,
    "I love thee true."

'She took me to her elfin grot,
    And there she wept, and sighed full sore,
And there I shut her wild, wild eyes
    With kisses four.

'And there she lullèd me asleep,
And there I dreamed—ah! woe betide!—
The latest dream I ever dreamed
    On the cold hill's side.

'I saw pale kings, and princes too,
    Pale warriors, death pale were they all;
They cried—"La belle Dame sans Merci
    Hath thee in thrall!"

'I saw their starved lips in the gloam
With horrid warning gapèd wide,
And I awoke, and found me here,
On the cold hill's side.

'And this is why I sojourn here
Alone and palely loitering,
Though the sedge is withered from the lake,
And no birds sing.'

This has many points in common with *The Ancient Mariner*. It is a narrative poem; it is in something like a ballad form; it has similar qualities of suggestion and concentrated power. Beauty and evil are closely allied; the medieval setting and the air of extreme unreality set off, rather than obscure, the poem's sinister suggestion. It is clearly a magical poem, and magic is thought of as having the power to make things happen. In *La Belle Dame* Keats was simply re-telling an old tale of unearthly and sinister beauty; he was obsessed with a sense of doomed and hopeless love, and in creating his poem, or conjuring it from his imagination, he was striving to exorcize the terrible power in whose grip he felt himself being overcome.

In both *The Ancient Mariner* and *La Belle Dame* we are aware of something quite different from prose, a use of language far removed from its use as normal statement. The actual form of the words, their varied and subtle acoustic qualities, the very shape and sound of the poem have an importance inseparable from the poem itself. It has, if you like, organic shape. It is difficult to get away from the idea of a natural form. You may say, 'A flower is not anything the flower *means*, or states, it is simply itself, its form—shape, colour, texture, smell.' 'A rose is a rose is a rose'—that is, itself and nothing else. It is impossible to think of a rose as being meaningless and without purpose or significance. So strongly have people felt this about a rose that they have ascribed to it all sorts of symbolic meanings. Now a poem is not a rose, but it has elements of the rose's self-sufficiency, its inexpressible significance, its unquestionable identity. Another, perhaps closer, parallel would be the song of a bird, since that, unlike a flower, cannot be experienced all at once: it begins and ends; like a poem, it exists in a dimension of time. Naturalists may agree about the *purpose* of a bird's song, for mating or for warning, or whatever it may be. But they do not know what its *meaning* is: they cannot tell why the song of one bird is different from that of another; why the same bird may have more than one song. Whatever the purpose of the song, the meaning is simply the song itself. A poem is not a bird's song, any more than it is a rose. But if it has not something of this quality of self-sufficiency, it is not a true poem and might as well have been presented as prose.

A. E. Housman went so far as to say, 'Poetry is not the thing said but a way of saying it.' In other words, meaning is of no importance; form is all-important. I don't think we can go this far. Poetry is the thing said *and* a way of saying it; or to put it another way, poetry is a way of saying *it* and nothing else. Form is an essential element in poetry, inseparable from meaning, and the identity of form and meaning is much closer than it can ever be, or need ever be, in prose.

We have looked at two examples of poetry which are very obviously poems and nothing else: I have chosen them on purpose for their contrast with prose and for the strength of their suggestion. They well illustrate the idea that poetry is verse plus magic. Other examples will be less easy to recognize as poetry. Can there be poems without magic? Essentially I believe not, but the magical element may be very small—what chemical analysts call a 'trace'. We shall look at poems which will seem, and which perhaps are, very little removed from prose, or versified prose. For the present it is all we can do to recognize and note the obvious differences. We must be able to recognize the difference between land and sea, even though we sometimes stand in a waste of shoals and sand-flats which seem to be neither. It is not necessary for a poem to contain exalted or romantic language to possess the magic of true poetry. Here, to end this chapter, is a passage of anonymous folk poetry written almost like a doggerel rhyme, yet having the concentrated force of a witch's curse. It is perhaps the utterance of a woman inspired to fury and despair by a man who betrayed every promise he had made. Who can say whether it was composed with deliberate artistry—as the measured, accusing note of the rhythm suggests—or simply grew, each image from the one before, as naturally and inevitably as the flower unfolding from the bulb?

> A man of words and not of deeds
> Is like a garden full of weeds;
> And when the weeds begin to grow,
> It's like a garden full of snow;
> And when the snow begins to fall,
> It's like a bird upon the wall;
> And when the bird away does fly,
> It's like an eagle in the sky;
> And when the sky begins to roar,
> It's like a lion at the door;
> And when the door begins to crack,
> It's like a stick across your back;
> And when your back begins to smart,
> It's like a penknife in your heart;
> And when your heart begins to bleed,
> You're dead, and dead, and dead indeed.

CHAPTER 5

POETRY AS SURPRISE

Most of what I, or any other writer, can say about a poem is likely to give the impression that it is something printed on paper. I want to insist that this is not altogether the truth. The printing on the paper is really a poem at second hand. It would be easier to see this if we were talking about painting or sculpture. When a writer on art wants to talk about a painting, he can print a small reproduction of it, either in colour or in black and white; and you know that this reproduction is not the actual painting. It is the same with music: books about music contain musical illustrations, and these are meant to be heard inside the head, as a kind of sound-picture of something you might hear in a concert hall. But with a poem it is different. I don't mean simply that a printed word is a notation for a spoken sound: true, it is this; but it is also something more: it is a notation for an object or an idea. This may seem obvious when you think about it, but it is often forgotten.

If a poem is not simply printed words on a page, or a notation for a series of spoken sounds, what is it? It is most helpful at this point, I think, to regard a poem as an event. At best, it is a magical event; and at worst it is only the feeble shadow of an event, or, if you like, an event that doesn't happen. The series of words represented by printing on the paper together makes a representation of an incident or event which takes place in the mind of the poet. The poem doesn't simply describe or relate an event in the poet's mind; it is itself an event. It doesn't happen in the poet's mind or anywhere else until it is written down, or at any rate composed in the poet's mind. Nobody can generalize about the way in which every poet writes. But I think it is true to say that usually some sort of disturbance happens in the poet's mind, and this takes shape as an event which can be communicated to others through the medium of the written word. A thunderstorm is an event which takes place in the atmosphere as the result of an electrical disturbance. Electric charges build up in the atmosphere until their force is released as lightning and thunder. A poem can occur when some sort of force or pressure builds up in the poet's mind and demands release in the form of a poetic event. Its appearance need not be sudden or explosive like a thunderclap; it may be slow and gradual. Nor, I must add, does this describe *all* kinds of poem; but I think it describes many of the best.

Until the poem has formed itself in the poet's mind—and it is unlikely to form itself completely except during the actual process of composition—the poet cannot be absolutely certain what he is going to write. Once it has been discharged from his mind, it takes its place in the series of events which go to make up the sum of all poetry. The reader to whose consciousness the new event is communicated will not get from the poem exactly the experience that built up in the poet's mind before he wrote it. But if the poem is a good one—or, to put it in another way, if the event is charged with magic—he and countless other readers can receive from it a shock or surprise. This is the shock of having a new experience. The reader's experience has been permanently enlarged.

Of course this is not the whole truth about poetry, or anything like it. But people so often write about poems as if they were just interesting thoughts dressed up in flowery language, that it is necessary to press the point I have been making. A schoolboy recently described poetry as 'All hey nonny nonny and bloody daffodils', and it is this school view of poetry that we need to get away from. In saying that a poem is an event, I want to insist that it is not just a mental exercise, to tease the brain, like a crossword puzzle; it is something which often seems to have more of a physical than an intellectual effect. On this point we have the testimony of more than one poet. Housman, for instance, says:

Poetry indeed seems to me more physical than intellectual. . . . Experience has taught me, when I am shaving of a morning, to keep watch over my thoughts, because, if a line of poetry strays into my memory, my skin bristles so that the razor ceases to act. This particular symptom is accompanied by a shiver down the spine; there is another which consists in a constriction of the throat and a precipitation of water to the eyes; and there is a third which I can only describe by borrowing a phrase from one of Keats' last letters, where he says, speaking of Fanny Brawne, 'Everything that reminds me of her goes through me like a spear'. The seat of this sensation is the pit of the stomach.

Before Housman's time, the American poet Emily Dickinson made a similar discovery for herself:

If I read a book and it makes my whole body so cold no fire can ever warm me, I know that is poetry. If I feel physically as if the top of my head were taken off, I know that is poetry. These are the only ways I know it. Is there any other way?

Housman and Emily Dickinson, you may say, were poets, not ordinary readers. But Emily Dickinson's friend Susan Gilbert was no poet, and she experienced the same feeling. Writing to Emily Dickinson about her stanza beginning 'Safe in their alabaster chambers', she said: 'I always go to the fire and get warm after thinking of it, but I never *can* again.'

In short, certain poems—not all of them—if read with proper concentration and discovered at the right moment in your life, can strike you with the shock of an actual physical experience. This does not perhaps happen very often; but no habitual reader of poetry is altogether immune from this kind of effect. After quoting the line by Milton, 'Nymphs and shepherds, dance no more', Housman said:

What is it that can draw tears, as I know it can, to the eyes of more readers than one? What in the world is there to cry about? Why have the mere words the physical effect of pathos when the sense of the passage is blithe and gay? I can only say, because they are poetry, and find their way to something in man which is obscure and latent, something older than the present organization of his nature . . .

Housman is here generalizing a personal experience. In his case the answer to the question 'What is there to cry about?' is not hard to find. He was what we should regard as a very literary reader of poetry; he was a classical scholar, and the words 'Nymphs and shepherds' would call up for him the whole half-imaginary pagan world of the Greek pastoral poet Theocritus. This world was one of ideal happiness, and it had long since vanished. 'Dance no more' suggests innocent pleasures gone for ever. We know that Housman was an intensely melancholy man, oppressed with a sense of lost innocence and thoughtless pleasure. As a young man, I visited him once, very briefly, in his rooms in Cambridge, and I recall the austere and chilly engraving of *Melancolia* by Dürer which hung just inside his door. To such a man the thought of happy innocence long vanished might indeed bring tears when expressed in Milton's melodious syllables. Compressed into only six short words, all the suggestion, all the pathos behind this thought might burst upon the mind of the poet-reader with the force of a shock. Perhaps you are not oppressed with a sense of lost innocence; perhaps you haven't read Theocritus, and know or care nothing about nymphs and shepherds. Then Milton's line will mean little to you. That doesn't mean you are deficient in sensibility and unresponsive to poetry. It means simply that you will have to find satisfaction in other poems or other poets. I have said that a poem is an event: it is also a transaction between you and the poet. Every reader is different from every other, and the same poem will affect each reader differently. The best poems are those which can make the profoundest impression on the greatest number and variety of readers over the longest period.

Every reader is different; but all readers have characteristics in common. This common element we may call humanity. It is through common humanity that a poet speaks to readers in other places and at other times than his own. He is peculiarly fitted to do so because the medium in which he works is language; and language is the bond between different members of the same human species. The words 'home', 'love', 'death', 'life', 'pity', 'peace' have large elements in common in the minds of all readers; yet each word means something slightly different in every single mind. Even simpler concepts such as 'face', 'book' and 'mirror' produce different images in the minds of different readers. A statement such as 'I look into my glass' (Hardy) or 'Faith is a fine invention' (Emily Dickinson) or 'The paths of glory lead but to the grave' (Gray) will have in the mind of each reader a basic core of similarity and at the same time call up vastly different images and associations. It is the property of a poem then, to appeal to the common humanity of all readers and at the same time to give each a different experience. What picture strikes your inner eye when you read De la Mare's line 'Very old are the

woods'? If you have never been outside a city, the picture may be
a vague one; it may be no more than a recollection of a painting
hanging on the wall in some room you are, or were, familiar with.
In my mind the line is inseparable from the tall, solemn beech-
woods which surrounded the home where I grew up. The trees in
my wood are grey-trunked, straight, and bathed in pale green
filtered sunlight. Your trees may be gloomy pines, red cedars or
spreading oaks. You might say that the poet generalizes and the
reader particularizes, and this makes a bond between them. If the
poet is too minute, too detailed and particular, he may lose his
hold on the reader; what he is writing may be too much like a
versified guide-book, and nothing is left to the reader's imagination. The poem makes no demands on the reader, who thus loses
interest. But when Shirley writes the line 'Death lays his icy hand
on kings', he stimulates the imagination because he leaves you to
fill in the details of his picture of icy-handed Death and of the
kings it strikes down. The poet makes a general statement that
even the greatest in the land are mortal, and puts it in such a form
as to stimulate the reader's imagination to fill in the picture.

I have quoted two poets, Housman and Emily Dickinson, as
testifying to the physical shock which poems can administer. The
testimony of poets is always worth hearing. Keats had something
to say about the point I have just been discussing. He says:

If poetry comes not as naturally as leaves to a tree, it had better not
come at all. . . . It should surprise by a fine excess, and not by singu-
larity; it should strike the reader as a wording of his own highest
thoughts, and appear almost a remembrance.

There seems to be a contradiction here. A poem should appear
to be a natural growth; it should also appear as something the
reader had already thought or experienced; yet it should *surprise*
by a fine excess. If it is natural, you may say, how can it be
excessive? If it strikes you as 'almost a remembrance', how can it
surprise? Keats here lights on one of the mysteries or paradoxes of
poetry. A shock is the more effective for not being wholly unexpected. A thing cannot really surprise you if it is incredible.
You have to feel, as soon as you are aware of it, that it had to
happen. When we read Emily Dickinson's four lines,

> Presentiment is that long shadow on the lawn
> Indicative that suns go down,
> The notice to the startled grass
> That darkness is about to pass

we are at first disconcerted by so strange a way of speaking; yet our surprise at its apparent oddity immediately gives place to a recognition of the rightness of the poet's observation. We see in our mind's eye some green lawn that we know or have known, with the long shadows of evening cutting across the sunlit turf. To Emily Dickinson this shadow was a presentiment of coming darkness, and we share her sense of chill foreboding. How could we feel this if the feeling were not already present at least in our subconscious mind? I cannot speak for every reader. Perhaps you have not experienced such a feeling. But to me at least the lines strike me as a wording of my own thoughts about shadows on the lawn. We may leave it at that, or we may take it further and say that Emily Dickinson was peculiarly subject to fear of the dark, because it was associated with death. Death was an ever-present fear, making the life she loved precarious in the extreme. 'Startled grass' seems at first an odd phrase, until we realize that she momentarily identifies herself with the grass, as she often did with objects in nature, and it is she who is startled by the passing (that is, passing over) of night. In this way the phrase both surprises by a fine excess and at the same time reveals itself as perfectly natural. She is a poet who is continually surprising by excess, yet satisfying by the justness and truth of her paradoxical utterances.

> Success is counted sweetest
> By those who ne'er succeed

and

> Exultation is the going
> Of an inland soul to sea

and

> One need not be a chamber to be haunted——

it is the combination of surprise and naturalness, of strangeness and truth which delights us in such poems as these. But as Keats saw, the two qualities must go together. Poetry which has no surprise cannot attract our attention; poetry which has no appearance of naturalness, but is continuously odd, cannot hold it for long.

The witches who greet Macbeth when he first appears gain his attention and exert their malign influence over him because they startle his inmost, hardly articulate thoughts by addressing him thus: 'All hail, Macbeth, that shalt be king hereafter!' Similarly a poet secures and holds your interest by letting you know what you are half thinking already, and expressing it in a new and surprising way. It follows, then, that there is a similar paradox about the poet himself. He shares the thoughts and feelings of the reader, indeed he anticipates them, so that he is endowed with a full share of common humanity. Yet if he were not at the same time different from the reader, he would have no hold over him, no power to surprise and satisfy him. What is it that makes a poet different from other people, and also the same?

CHAPTER 6

WHAT IS A POET?

What is a poet? This is one of the questions asked by Wordsworth and Coleridge in their famous preface to the second edition of *Lyrical Ballads*. We shall be considering their answer later. First, let us think about what we mean when we ask such a question. It sounds as if we thought that all poets were similar in some obvious way, like policemen or soldiers. But if we could line up twenty poets of different periods in one room, we should be hard put to it to recognize them as having the same nature or profession. Six of our poets might be, respectively, a farm labourer, a prosperous banker, a neatly dressed publisher, a domesticated young woman, a clergyman and a shy, unsuccessful schoolmaster. Clearly there is nothing in the outward appearance, social status or professional character of such a group to indicate that all are poets. Some poets have come from the humblest classes of society, some from the hereditary aristocracy. Some have other jobs all their lives, others have no means of support except their writing. Certainly there is no *profession* of poet, in the generally understood sense; all we can say for certain is that a poet is one who writes poetry. Have poets anything else in common?

It has been said that poets are born and not made. Can we truthfully say that the poetic character descends on a man at birth, and that there is nothing hereditary in it? It is surprising how many poets have been the sons of minor poets or versifiers. Browning, Hopkins and Robert Graves all had fathers who wrote minor verse. Moreover, a few poets gave birth to children who were talented in the same way. Coleridge's three children, Hartley, Derwent and Sara, all published poems, and those of Hartley at least were not unworthy to have been written by a child of Coleridge. On the other hand, it is possible to mention a far greater number of poets who had nothing poetic in their parentage

—Clare, Hardy, Shelley, Keats and Pope, to name only five. Some, it is true, came from literary families, like Milton, Yeats and Arnold. But there have been many thousands of bookish households in which no poet has been born.

Since it is impossible, then, to ascribe poetic talent to any firm hereditary principle, is it true to say that poets are made, not born? We have only to think of the thousands upon thousands of volumes of uninspired and stillborn verse that have been published, all the efforts of ambitious and industrious scribblers to get themselves numbered among the poets, to realize that nothing can make a man a poet if he has no inborn talent. Nevertheless it is true that exceptional poetic gifts usually show themselves later than a gift for painting or music. For every one poet who achieves real distinction, there are hundreds who wrote promising verse as children. Yet a real child prodigy in poetry has scarcely ever existed, if at all. The qualities that make a poet may appear early, and may be very widespread, but if they are to come to maturity and fruition, other qualities are necessary; and one of these is certainly application, study and concentration on the craft of poetry. Perhaps Ben Jonson was nearest the mark when he said, writing of Shakespeare after his death, 'For a good poet's made as well as born'. In other words, application is necessary if the inborn poetical faculty is to mature.

When Pope, as a grown man, wrote 'I lisped in numbers, for the numbers came', he meant that as a child he had a natural gift for verse. He deliberately spent the whole of his life polishing and perfecting this talent. He tells us also that his teacher, Walsh, urged him as a boy to cultivate correctness and refine his verse to the highest pitch imaginable. Others were fired by youthful ambition to achieve the rank of great poets and earn lasting fame. What is not so clear is why they should desire this. True, poets were once held in great honour by their fellow men. But this is not so common nowadays; yet there is no lack of candidates for poetic fame. Certainly the trade of poet is conspicuously ill-paid, and few enter it for material reasons. Undoubtedly many poets enjoy the praise and encouragement of those whose judgement they respect, but this is by no means universal. Emily Dickinson and Hopkins received very little encouragement, yet continued to write poetry during the greater part of their mature lives. They expected and won almost no recognition. Clare continued to write long after the praise that had greeted his first book of poems lapsed into silence. Blake's genius was similarly unrecognized. Clearly, something more than material rewards and earthly fame urges a poet to write. We must conclude that there is something in the nature of a man to make him a poet, and this something is not connected with either his birth and social position or his concern with his life in the world as he knows it. He may remain poor and neglected, like Blake, or he may achieve affluence and worldly success, like Tennyson, but this has little to do with his initial urge to be a poet.

We may admit that many poets have wished to achieve fame or recognition for their work; Keats openly sought fame, and Clare, an obscure farm labourer's son, undoubtedly strove to emerge from obscurity by means of his poems. But the quality of ambition, which is discoverable in many young poets, hardly explains their choice of a vocation. Many who began as writers of verse have turned to other forms of literature, such as fiction, or to other professions, such as politics, medicine or the church. So we have to ask, not only 'What makes a poet in the first place?' but also 'What keeps him a poet despite the opportunities and temptations to turn into something else?'

Let us look at the answer given by Wordsworth and Coleridge.

What is a poet? To whom does he address himself? And what language is to be expected from him?—He is a man speaking to men: a man, it is true, endowed with more lively sensibility, more enthusiasm and tenderness, who has a greater knowledge of human nature, and a more comprehensive soul, than are supposed to be common among mankind; a man pleased with his own passions and volitions, and who rejoices more than other men in the spirit of life that is in him; delighting to contemplate similar volitions and passions as manifested in the goings on of the Universe, and habitually impelled to create them where he does not find them. . . . He has acquired a greater readiness and power in expressing what he thinks and feels. . . .

A bold claim is made here. Can we agree that poets are so very different from other men? Have they more lively sensibilities, more understanding of human nature, more comprehensive souls, and more powerful imaginations than the rest of mankind? Leaving this aside for the moment, I think we can agree that a poet is 'pleased with his own passions and volitions' and that he 'rejoices more than other men in the spirit of life that is in him'. In other words, he not only has a marked capacity for sheer animal delight in life; he takes pleasure in this capacity, and rejoices in the sheer gratification of his instincts. We may agree that he is acutely sensitive, and that he has a powerful imagination—that is, the capacity to project himself beyond his immediate surroundings. Now these qualities are not confined to poets. They are the possession, in greater or less degree, of most human beings. Children are commonly endowed with sensitive natures and a capacity for animal pleasure. In this they are like poets, and the true poet retains something of these child-like qualities. But a poet has something which not every child possesses—'a greater readiness and power in expressing what he thinks and feels'. As Robert Graves puts it, in the lines which begin his poem *The Cool Web*.

> Children are dumb to say how hot the day is,
> How hot the scent is of the summer rose,
> How dreadful the black wastes of evening sky,
> How dreadful the tall soldiers drumming by.

That is, children are acutely sensitive to physical sensations, but they are 'dumb' in expressing their awareness. A poet, by some inexplicable hereditary, environmental or physiological accident, is articulate where the child is dumb: he possesses a greater readiness and power in expressing himself. This is not, of course, the whole of the matter. Poets express much more than just physical awareness of their environment; but this capacity to articulate their sensations is the basis of their special nature.

Basically it is to be doubted whether poets possess the exceptional qualities claimed for them by Wordsworth and Coleridge; if they did, it would be by cultivation, by the continual striving for the power of articulation, by the development of exceptional powers of speech and exceptional ability to use words. We would hesitate nowadays to make such claims for poets as were once made. We would have to admit that there are many besides poets who have an acute awareness of physical sensations, a profound understanding of human nature; there are many besides poets who are 'pleased with their own passions and volitions', and who are endowed with imaginative power. We would admit, moreover, that 'a poet is a man speaking to men'; and this is where the difference begins. For he cannot speak to men unless he has a peculiar power of articulate speech, an exceptional command of language. It seems to me to be a more acceptable claim for poets that they are *not* different from others except in this respect. They are simply like others, only more so. I believe that a true poet resents being thought peculiar and 'different'. He would prefer to be thought of as a man in the fullest sense, but withdrawn from the rest of the world by a capacity, partly innate and partly trained, to speak to others, and by a recognition of the responsibilities which this entails.

A poet is, in short, something of a 'sport', to use the scientific term. He is the same as the rest of the species, with one characteristic abnormally developed. The only sense in which a poet is different from others is that the most characteristically human faculty—the faculty to create and use language—is in him over-developed.

What first distinguished a poet from other children or young people begins as an interest in language for its own sake—the experience of sensations as language, rather than as purely physical phenomena. This interest may develop into an obsession, so that to have any experience not reducible to words becomes a source of dissatisfaction, even of pain.

To say that a poet prefers words to life is a half-truth. Rather, life is meaningless until it is experienced in articulate speech. He feels a compulsion to 'speak to men'—or at any rate, to put something into words which can be read by others if they want to.

Now this impulse or compulsion to apprehend experience as words is not confined to poets, at any rate in childhood. Indeed, every child wishes to express pleasure and pain, curiosity and feeling. But not every child wishes to do this in a permanent and compelling form. A potential poet not only takes pleasure in expressing his thoughts in interesting language; he enjoys similar expressions by others. All children enjoy the verbal sensations derived from nursery rhymes; a poet tries to recapture and repeat this pleasure by creating language-patterns of his own. He finds that, as others have made unique and lasting things out of words, he too can do so, according to the degree of his skill in using them. But interest, application and skill are not enough; an inner impulse to make new combinations is not enough. There must be what is called inspiration.

Inspiration is an unfashionable word, and the idea that poetry is inspired is frowned on by scientific critics, because it is something they cannot explain. The word 'inspiration' was once in common use, but has suffered devaluation. I don't apologize for using it, and I see no reason to try to find another word. To recognize its existence, it is not necessary to be able to define it. Some poets have claimed to write without it, but all true poets know what is meant by it and when it is present or absent in their work. A poet may try to express himself poetically, using all his skill and knowledge in the choice of language; the poem refuses to 'come'; nothing he writes satisfies him. The thing is no good and he tears it up in despair. Another time he seems to be aware of a kind of mental, almost physical excitement, which makes his work comparatively easy; the poem 'comes right' without much difficulty. Such a power often seems to come from outside, not from within himself. It seems to be independent of verbal skill. It is not something he has learned; it is something which has happened. This power, or faculty, is what is meant by inspiration. It cannot be induced voluntarily; it goes as swiftly as it comes. You may call this power irrational, or you may call it super-rational. To Housman it came at times when his intellect was at its most sluggish. It comes when mere reason is asleep. At such times a poet writes beyond his normal powers, at a pitch higher than he attains by his ordinary skill as a craftsman. He can never *make* himself write more than accomplished verse, clever imitations of true poetry. Only this inexplicable power, usually called inspiration, can make him write poetry.

Most people, according to their occupations, are obliged to use language purely rationally, for the purposes of prose: explanation, exposition, description, intelligible command or intellectual

D

argument. Children, savages and poets use language irrationally. Most of our communications with each other are made in
the language of reason. But poets know there is a language of
unreason which speaks to depths in human understanding beyond
reason. Civilized man has developed the faculty of reason to an
abnormal extent; scientific thought is rational thought at its most
advanced. If science is opposed to poetry, it is because poetry is
not wholly rational. Macaulay said, 'As civilization advances,
poetry almost necessarily declines.' But there is a child and a
savage in us all, and because the poet keeps open the channels of
communication in his own nature between adult civilized man and
the buried child and savage, he can reveal and draw on the hidden
irrationality in human nature.

No one thinks any longer that we can base our civilization
solely on reason; no one believes that the irrational impulses, both
destructive and creative, in human nature can be wholly sub-
dued. Even scientists are beginning to realize that it is un-
scientific to ignore the irrational element in humanity; it is
irrational to regard humanity as wholly rational.

As Emily Dickinson wrote:

> Much madness is divinest sense
> To a discerning eye—
> Much sense the starkest madness.

In former times poets were often regarded as mad. This was
simply a way of expressing the feeling that only poets were aware
of the forces of unreason and in contact with them through inspired speech. It is worth while to consider Theseus' words in
A Midsummer Night's Dream:

> The lunatic, the lover, and the poet
> Are of imagination all compact:
> One sees more devils than vast hell can hold,
> That is, the madman; the lover, all as frantic,
> Sees Helen's beauty in a brow of Egypt:
> The poet's eye, in a fine frenzy rolling,
> Doth glance from heaven to earth, from earth to heaven:
> And, as imagination bodies forth
> The forms of things unknown, the poet's pen

Turns them to shapes, and gives to airy nothing
A local habitation and a name.
Such tricks hath strong imagination,
That, if it would but apprehend some joy,
It comprehends some bringer of that joy;
Or in the night, imagining some fear,
How easy is a bush supposed a bear!

It is because poets have something in common with lunatics that they were once regarded, and are perhaps still regarded, with suspicion. Plato wished to banish them from the ideal commonwealth, that is, the society based entirely on reason. But what is the use of such a society? What kind of sense does any civilization make if it has not the poetry of Aescyhlus and Sophocles, Catullus, Villon and Rimbaud, Shakespeare and Blake? For these are the men whose imagination made sense of a world which pure reason would turn into something merely mechanical. The successes of science are very real and very necessary to modern society; but modern society would be meaningless without the successes of unreason—art, comedy, music, poetry and altruism.

To mention Sophocles and Villon and Shakespeare brings us a long way, it seems, from common humanity. Yet who can doubt that Shakespeare was a man in the fullest sense of the word? He was a man who comprehended the thoughts and feelings and experiences of many more than just one man; he comprehended more human experience than any other man. He did so by and through his mastery of language. So immense is the range of experience comprised in *Hamlet* and *King Lear* that we sometimes forget that these plays consist of nothing but words. Through words Shakespeare became all men.

Nobody has framed a definition of the poet that can apply to every writer of poetry. But ideally it can be said that he is not unlike other men: he is like many different men, and separated from them only by an abnormally developed power of speech. While no one, however hard he applies himself, can be sure of becoming a poet, anyone can be born a potential poet. According to Dr Johnson, Dryden told his young relative, 'Cousin Swift, you will never be a poet.' This was because Swift had not much success at writing the kind of thing Dryden considered poetry, the kind of thing he wrote himself. Dryden did not live to see his cousin become a poet far more imaginative, humane and moving than ever he had been.

CHAPTER 7

KINDS OF POEM—1
Mother Goose Rhymes, Ballads

We have been talking in a very general way about poetry and poets. Now we must begin to discuss the many and various types of poem. To indicate the variety of these types, it is only necessary to name a few of them. Nursery rhymes (what are called in America Mother Goose rhymes), ballads, folk songs, epics, odes, sonnets, satires and parodies—all these must be discussed. It is true, I think—though some would deny it—that there is a common quality, poetry, which is to be found in all these different types; and we have tried in an earlier chapter to sketch out a definition. But we cannot for long consider poetry as a whole without thinking of the various kinds of poem.

Now all the poetry of a civilized community—and I am thinking here of the English-speaking community from the time when the English language as we know it was evolved—can be divided into two major categories: anonymous poems and poems written by individuals. Most poetry is now of the latter class. It is difficult to imagine any considerable addition to the great body of anonymous poems in English. This has to do with the spread of education and the growth of written records. For hundreds of years before the beginnings of poetry written by individuals whose names are known, there was in existence a vast oral culture and a body of poems handed down from one generation to another by word of mouth only. We may call this ballad literature. The authors of ballads were not remembered, and we can only conjecture who they were. This ballad tradition continued, side by side with the more literary tradition, right on into the nineteenth century, and it has existed wherever there have been considerable bodies of people to whom reading came with difficulty or not at all. Infants and young school children remain the last survivors of the oral tradition, and they still possess a body of rhymes and songs which, though most have now been collected and written down by scholars, are still handed down by word of mouth from one generation of children to the next.

Let us begin with infants—the youngest children, who learn rhymes from their mothers long before they are able to read. Every child learns *Little Boy Blue*, *Jack and Jill*, *Baa baa, Black Sheep* and *See-saw, Margery Daw*, as well as many others of these Mother Goose rhymes—so called because of the eighteenth-century collection, *Mother Goose's Melody*.

It is easy to dismiss these rhymes as mere childishness. That would be a mistake. For certain definite poetic reasons they form an excellent foundation for the taste of every English-speaking reader. Take, for instance:

> Hey diddle diddle,
> The cat and the fiddle,
>   The cow jumped over the moon;
> The little dog laughed
> To see such sport,
>   And the dish ran away with the spoon.

Nonsense, you might say, and quite unworthy of attention. But to begin with, the rhythm and the word-music are excellent. The rhyme is complete in itself, and although quite mad, has a sort of internal logic of its own. It may originally have been an occupational rhyme, designed to encourage children to eat up their dinner and make an empty plate. Children can be encouraged to do any task more quickly and willingly with the aid of a rhyme. Moreover, the rhyme is without sentimentality; the dog is given a certain human quality by being made to laugh, but there is no false sentiment about it. The idea of a cow jumping over the moon has just that touch of imaginative lunacy which appeals to a high-spirited child. The rhyme has an imperishable gaiety and careless-ness which has endeared it to generation after generation of child-ren. It seems to have been first printed two hundred years ago, but was probably in existence at least two hundred years before that.

It is the completeness of Mother Goose rhymes that makes them especially satisfying to children.

There was a crooked man, who walked a crooked mile,
He found a crooked sixpence upon a crooked stile;
He bought a crooked cat, which caught a crooked mouse,
And they all lived together in a little crooked house.

Here is a complete story—you might almost say, a life story—in miniature, which defiantly contradicts the laws of probability, and so appeals to a child's insatiable love of surprises.

Not all Mother Goose rhymes are so gay. Some have a note of cruelty, a hint of the callousness towards children and animals which was characteristic of an earlier generation. The three blind mice which have their tails cut off, the cat pushed into the well by little Tommy Green, the baby whose cradle falls from the broken bough in a high wind—such rhymes are hard to explain, unless we realize that the child mind is hard, factual, realistic and not at all given to humanitarian notions about the helplessness of small creatures. Perhaps the theme of *Three Blind Mice* acts as a harmless expression of those instincts of cruelty and fear which exist in the subconscious layers of the human mind—in the case of children not much below the surface.

There is probably a good deal of forgotten social and political history in the Mother Goose rhymes. Scholars claim to have identified the 'little Jack Horner' who congratulated himself on his share of the pie; the rhyme about Margery Daw may refer to the days of child labour in English factories, when a girl or boy might be employed for as little as a penny a day. But that is not the reason why these rhymes survive today. If you have ever seen a small girl on a see-saw chanting the Margery Daw rhyme to herself, you will realize that it is the perfect accompaniment to this time-honoured and ritual form of play. Many other rhymes were the accompaniment of games. But who bothers to think, when a group of three-year-olds are playing *Ring a Ring o' Roses*, that this rhyme was in origin a grim reminder of the days when in an outbreak of the plague sweet herbs were carried to ward off an attack, whose symptoms might be a rosy rash on the skin and a feverish chill ending in sudden death?

Whatever the origins of the Mother Goose rhymes—and it is certain that most of them were not written for children—but adopted by, or adapted for them—it is worth while to dwell for

a little longer on the poetic qualities which give them permanent
value. I have spoken of them as complete, concrete, and unsenti-
mental. They are also magical in form and often in theme. They
are rhythmically strong, without any affectation; the rhymes are
for the most part bold, though often only approximate, as befits
verses handed down by word of mouth. The ear is less scrupulous
than the eye in matters of rhyme.

> Oranges and lemons,
> Say the bells of St Clement's.
>
> You owe me five farthings,
> Say the bells of St Martin's.
>
> When will you pay me?
> Say the bells of Old Bailey.
>
> When I grow rich,
> Say the bells of Shoreditch.
>
> When will that be?
> Say the bells of Stepney.
>
> I'm sure I don't know,
> Says the great bell at Bow.

How very satisfying to the ear is this chime of old London
bells, yet no more than half of its couplets are strictly rhymed. We
may say that the anonymous author took a liberal view of rhyme,
and that in his hands language was a vigorous and organic thing,
not to be used pedantically, the servant and not the master of
sense.

It is this rigour of language which is the most valuable element
in the Mother Goose rhymes. One of the marks of literary writing,
as distinct from traditional poetry, is the use of adjectives. Take,
as an illustration, the first stanza of Gray's *Elegy*:

> The curfew tolls the knell of parting day,
>   The lowing herd winds slowly o'er the lea,
> The plowman homeward plods his weary way,
>   And leaves the world to darkness and to me.

In each of the first three lines there is an adjective which is not
strictly necessary. 'Parting' tells us nothing which is not in the

much stronger word 'knell'. In the second line the word 'lowing' certainly contributes atmosphere, and introduces an element of sound into an otherwise purely visual scene, but it could be dispensed with. In the third line 'weary' adds little that is not in the word 'plods'. So that if Gray had written his poem in a more compressed verse form—

> The curfew tolls the knell of day,
> The herd winds slowly o'er the lea,
> The plowman homeward plods his way
> And leaves the darkening world to me—

he would have said almost as much as is said in the longer verse form; but he would have given the lines a terseness and vigour which he was not really aiming at. The long-drawn-out, almost languid sound of the lines contributes to the atmosphere of the *Elegy*, but it adds nothing to its sense. If you compare this with *Hey diddle diddle*, quoted earlier, you will at once realize the economy and compression gained from the absence of adjectives. The only adjective, in fact, is the more or less neutral 'little' qualifying 'dog'. Throughout the Mother Goose rhymes this economy gives them vigour and directness often lacking in literary poetry.

But, you may say, such rhymes are trivial; these are not the qualities of great poetry. Yet these same qualities are evident in a body of poetry of far greater and more mature appeal, the anonymous ballads of the Middle Ages. I spoke of the imaginary 'author' of *Oranges and Lemons*, and it is worth while to stop and consider this question of authorship; for when we come to the traditional ballads, we are on very debatable ground. Some scholars used to maintain with considerable heat that the 'folk' was the author of the ballads; they believed in the theory of what was called 'communal authorship', according to which whole groups or communities of people spontaneously composed poems such as *Sir Patrick Spens* and *The Dæmon Lover*. This theory has long been abandoned; at the same time, the authorship of such poems must remain a tantalizing mystery. It is easier to believe that every ballad was originally composed by a single author, passed on from generation to generation, and altered and adapted in the process, while remaining essentially the original poem. This is attested by the fact that many versions of the same ballad existed in different parts of Britain and later America, all bearing a strong family resemblance, but each differing in minor or major particulars. The original author was almost certainly a professional minstrel or singing man, probably the descendant of a line of singers, gifted with exceptional creative talents.

The only difficulty about such a comparatively simple account is that the same ballad—or the same narrative in ballad form— turns up all over Europe, and even in the East, in the language of the country where it is found. It is equally difficult to believe that the same ballad was simultaneously composed in a number of languages, and alternatively that some prototype was consciously translated into a number of different tongues. Yet it seems that something like this must have happened, probably at a time when migrations of tribes took place on a vast scale.

In the ballad of *Edward*, for instance, the most celebrated versions recovered in Britain are in the Scottish dialect.

> 'Why does your brand sae drop wi' blude,
>   Edward, Edward?
> Why does your brand sae drop wi' blude,
>   And why sae sad gang ye, O?'

> 'O I hae kill'd my hawk sae gude,
>   Mither, mither;
> O I hae kill'd my hawk sae gude,
>   And I had nae mair byt he, O.'

The poem continues the dialogue between mother and son, in which the son finally confesses that it is not his hawk or his horse he has slain but his father, and that he acted on the evil advice of his mother, whom accordingly he curses. This sombre and tragic theme appears in many European languages, as well as in comparatively late American versions. It was evidently once part of a common western culture, perhaps deriving ultimately from the east, and broken up by the settlement of the various peoples into separate nation states.

Whatever the original authorship of the anonymous ballads, they remain the root and basis of English poetry. No one would wish that poets of today consciously imitated their outward form and style (though such imitation is not uncommon); but poets now and at all intervening times have been able to learn from the example of the nameless ballad-authors of the past. To begin with, the ballads employ the basic speech rhythms of the English tongue, heightened and formalized to suit a fixed purpose—the purpose of memorization and possibly adaptation to a known melody.

As I was walking all alane,
I heard twa corbies[1] making a mane:[2]
The tane unto the tother say,
'Whar sall we gang and dine today?'

'In behint yon auld fail-dyke,[3]
I wot there lies a new-slain knight;
And naebody kens that he lies there
But his hawk, his hound and his lady fair.

'His hound is to the hunting gane,
His hawk to fetch the wild-fowl hame,
His lady's ta'en anither mate,
So we may mak our dinner sweet.

'Ye'll sit on his white hause-bane,[4]
And I'll pike out his bonny blue e'en;
Wi' ae lock o' his gowden hair
We'll theek[5] our nest when it grows bare.

'Mony a one for him maks mane,
But nane sall ken whar he is gane;
O'er his white banes when they are bare,
The wind sall blaw for ever mair.'

The rhythm is strongly marked, yet perfectly natural; the ordinary movement of English speech is not forced or falsified. The language is vigorous and economical. The stark cheerlessness of the desolate scene is conveyed, not by the use of atmospheric adjectives but by the selection of suitable details. I have chosen to quote this ballad because it is a peculiarly successful example of balladry at its most powerful. Many ballads are longer because the

[1] ravens   [2] moan   [3] old turf wall   [4] neck-bone   [5] thatch

narrative is given in greater detail, though not necessarily with less economy. What we have in *The Twa Corbies* is not so much an account of foul play as an ironic reflection on it, in which use is made of the traditional belief that evil deeds were witnessed and reported on by birds and beasts. This same belief, that a murderer will be betrayed by the birds, is expressed by Macbeth when he is reflecting on his assassination of Duncan.

The traditional ballads are the record of those things which aroused the emotions of our ancestors, the emotions of wonder, fear, pity or rage. If you or I see something which arouses our emotions, a street fire or a road accident, our impulse is to rush off and tell someone about it. It is partly, perhaps, that we are possessed by the desire to be the first to recount it and so gain a passing notoriety; but equally we are overcome by fear—it is as if we felt ourselves to be in possession of a guilty secret—and we feel compelled to unburden ourselves of the fear and guilt by sharing it. It is partly this instinct which was responsible for the composition and transmission of the ballads. The events which our ancestors desired to celebrate or perpetuate were battles, crimes of passion or revenge, magical happenings involving the supernatural. Such events are still the stock-in-trade of sensational journalism; but we have lost the art of, and also the need for, balladry, and we no longer create masterpieces of oral poetry. The reason of course is partly the speed and ease of communication. People no longer take the time to compose masterpieces; we prefer to get our news hot from the radio or mass-circulation papers, within a few hours. We have other satisfactions, and no one would bewail not living in the Middle Ages. At the same time, it is important, if we are to enjoy poetry to the full, to realize what our ancestors had that we have lost.

I don't want to imply that all ballads are masterpieces. Some are tedious, pedestrian and uninspired. At the head of our ballad literature we rightly place such poems as *Sir Patrick Spens*, *Clerk Saunders*, *The Wife of Usher's Well*, *The Dæmon Lover* and *True Thomas*. But the Robin Hood ballads, once extremely popular, are not for the most part in this class. The narrative is exciting enough, but we are nearer to mere reporting in verse and a good way removed from magical or suggestive poetry.

A word must be said about the survival of the hundreds of traditional English and Scottish ballads which the modern reader has to choose from. Since they were originally transmitted by word of mouth, they would undoubtedly have perished but for the interest of antiquaries and scholars, especially in the eighteenth century. It is true that, with the invention of printing, the selling of broadsides and ballad-sheets became popular and widespread. These sheets were purveyed for the profit of printers by ballad-singers and pedlars at fairs and markets, and were eagerly bought by anyone who could read and so entertain his less literate friends. There is a fine scene in Shakespeare's *A Winter's Tale* that depicts ballad-selling by the vagrant Autolycus. Here the country people show themselves anxious to learn of new and startling events through the medium of ballad-sheets. Much of the material thus circulated was of inferior quality, and a very great deal of it must have perished. But during the seventeenth and eighteenth centuries the surviving sheets were sought after by collectors, so that by the middle of the eighteenth century Bishop Percy was able to publish a considerable volume of anonymous ballad literature. It is also evident from numerous references in Shakespeare that there was a large stock-in-trade of popular ballads and songs familiar to people in general. It was partly an interest in these references which led to the growth of antiquarian interest in balladry. Sir Walter Scott made an important collection of ballads from the country people of the Scots border. These he took down from the singing of people who could not read, and simply repeated their songs from memory. By the end of the nineteenth century a considerable body of published ballads was in existence, and on these the American scholar Francis James Child of Harvard based his monumental edition of over three hundred *English and Scottish Popular Ballads*. It is probable that every important ballad of anonymous, traditional origin has now been printed, so that we are in no danger of losing this supreme poetic inheritance. Nevertheless, it is worth remembering that the oral tradition, which goes back to scarcely recorded times, is still not quite dead. In the remoter parts of Britain—mainly in Ireland and the west and north of Scotland—as well as in the more unfrequented parts of the United States, versions of some of the old ballads are still heard and recorded by ballad and folk-song collectors. These are taken down from the lips of country people who learned their songs, not from books, gramophone or radio, but from the mouths of older people to whom they had been handed on in earlier times. It has to be admitted, however, that the days when ballad singing was an active and flourishing pursuit are long past. The tradition has almost died, but the ballads themselves remain, as fresh, moving and direct as ever.

CHAPTER 8

KINDS OF POEM—2
Folk Song

Another branch of balladry which is very popular today, as it was hundreds of years ago, is what is rather loosely called *folk song*. Let us not spend too long trying to define this term. It is now applied both to old, genuine songs of anonymous authorship sung by country people centuries ago, and to modern imitations in the old style. We can all recognize the type. A favourite way of making a commercial success in Tin Pan Alley is to take an old song and hot it up for use by dance bands and 'pop' singers. Such commercial hits as *All Round my Hat* and *On Top of Old Smoky* are both songs of ancient origin. Whether this commercialization is a good thing or not does not concern us here: my own view is that you can't generalize. If the modernization is well done, it would be pedantic to quarrel with it. These are the songs of the people, and it is up to the people to do what they like with them. For one characteristic of folk songs is their adaptability and variety. All really popular folk songs occur in various versions in different parts of the English-speaking world. There is no 'correct' version; there are only good and bad versions.

Let us take an example, well known in America, *The Streets of Laredo*, probably existing in its present form from the days of the cowboys, about a hundred years ago.

As I rode out in the streets of Laredo,
As I rode out in Laredo one day,
I spied a young cowboy so brave, young and handsome,
Dressed up in white linen and cold as the clay.

'I see by your outfit that you are a cowboy,'
These words he did say as I boldly stepped by.
'Come sit down beside me and hear my sad story,
I was shot in the breast and I know I must die.

"'Twas once in the saddle I used to go dashing,
'Twas once in the saddle I used to go gay;
I first took to drinking and then to card-playing,
Got shot in the breast and I'm dying today.

'Then beat the drum slowly and play the fife lowly,
And play a dead march as you carry me along,
Take me to the prairie and throw the sod o'er me,
For I'm a young cowboy although I've done wrong.

'Let sixteen gamblers come carry my coffin
And six pretty maidens come bear up my pall.
Lay bunches of roses all over my coffin,
Lay roses to deaden the clods as they fall.'

We beat the drum slowly and played the fife lowly
And bitterly wept as we carried him along
For we all loved our comrade so brave, young and handsome
We all loved the cowboy although he'd done wrong.

This is an excellent song, usually sung to a haunting tune probably of Irish origin. Those who think the song inappropriate to cowboy life don't know its origin in the Britain of earlier times.

One day as I strolled down the Royal Albion,
Dark was the morning and cold was the day,
Then who should I spy but one of my shipmates,
Draped in a blanket and colder than clay.

This is the beginning of a song usually known as *The Sailor Cut Down in his Prime*, and the reason why he was cut down is that he died of a venereal disease. This fact is glossed over in many versions of the song, and also in the American cowboy song, because of the strength of Puritan tradition. There is still another English version, which may be yet earlier, *The Young Girl Cut Down in her Prime*.

As I was a-walking down by the seaside,
As I was a walking there one day,
Oh who should I spy but my own daughter Mary
Wrapped up in some flannel some hot summer's day.

This is enough to suggest the variety and adaptability of folk songs. Countless other examples could be given.

There is about genuine folk song a simplicity, directness and naturalness often lacking in other kinds of poetry. The best songs are part of the rural culture of pre-industrial days, and were kept alive by singers engaged in agricultural occupations. Many of the best singers were women engaged in monotonous tasks, like spinning or milking, or by men at harvest suppers and other seasonal festivities. The subjects of folk song are many, but the most universally popular in Britain are love songs. Love and courtship, though not usually marriage, are the most universal and basic themes; and the sorrows of young girls betrayed by love provide the inspiration of many of the most moving.

Shortly after the great American scholar, Child, had made his collection of popular English and Scottish ballads from printed sources, an Englishman, Cecil Sharp, began a thorough study of folk songs taken down from the lips of country people in Somerset. He was not the first of those who collected songs in this way, but he was probably the most persistent and the most successful, both in the number and in the variety of the versions he took down, both words and melodies. His editing of the words for the English market was less successful, because it involved the suppression of much of the true character of the songs, many of which are frank and wanton. But he preserved his manuscripts unaltered for later editors. He is doubly important because he was also a pioneer in the collection of songs in the United States. The book he edited with Maud Karpeles, *English Folk Songs of the Southern Appalachians*, is a work of the utmost importance, showing as it did how many English songs had been transported to America and preserved in the memories of country people.

The first song which Sharp took down from the lips of a Somerset countryman was *The Seeds of Love*. No wonder it excited his curiosity and his thirst for further finds. It is a song of indestructible beauty, whose qualities are quite different from those we connect with more literary poetry.

> I sowed the seeds of love,
> And I sowed them in the spring,
> In April and May and June likewise
> When the small birds sweetly sing.

My garden was planted well
With sweet flowers everywhere,
But I had not the liberty to choose for myself
The flower that I loved so dear.

The gardener standing by
I asked to choose for me;
He chose me the violet, the lily and the pink,
But these I refused all three.

The violet I did not like
Because it fades so soon;
The lily and the pink I did overthink,
But vowed I would wait till June.

In June is the red-red rose,
And that's the flower for me,
So I pulled and I plucked at the red rosebud
Till I gained the willow-tree.

Oh the willow-tree will twist,
And the willow-tree will twine,
And I wish I was in that young man's arms
That first had this heart of mine.

It is impossible to be even approximately sure when this song began. It has the quality of timelessness, and springs from a rural culture in which the symbolism of herbs and flowers was common knowledge. It is supposed to be sung by a young woman who has made a fatal choice and found that the fruit of passion is betrayal. In the garden of life she has planted the seeds of those qualities from which she must in time make her choice; the violet for modesty, the lily for purity, the pink for courtesy and polite breeding. She rejects the advice of the gardener, whom we may take to be Conscience or Good Counsel, and chooses instead the red rose of reckless passion. What she gains in the end is the willow-tree—that is, the weeping willow of remorse for betrayal in love.

Many folk songs treat of amorous adventures in a more light-hearted, as well as a more outspoken way. Here are the words of *Strawberry Fair* as originally sung, before they were turned into the pretty trifle sung in schools everywhere. This also gives a good example of the kind of chorus lines which occur in so many folk songs. These choruses or refrains often seem to be pure nonsense, but they are evidently intended as imitations of an instrumental accompaniment, chorused by the audience to the sound of a fiddle, while the soloist took breath. The use of Freudian symbolism in this song preserves it from obvious coarseness.

> As I was a-going to Strawberry Fair,
>   Rifol, ri-fol, riddle, tol-de-lido,
> I saw a fair maiden of beauty rare,
>   Tol-de-dee,
> I saw a fair maid selling her ware
> As I went on to Strawberry Fair,
>   Rifol, ri-fol, riddle tol-de-lido.
>
> Oh, pretty fair maiden, I prithee tell,
> My pretty fair maid, what do you sell?
> Oh, come tell me truly, my sweet damsel,
> As you go on to Strawberry Fair.
>
> Oh, I have a lock that doth lack a key,
> Oh, I have a lock, sir, she did say.
> If you have a key, then come this way,
> As we go on to Strawberry Fair.
>
> Between us I reckon that when we met,
> The key to the lock it was well set,
> The key to the lock it well did fit,
> As we went on to Strawberry Fair.
>
> Oh, would that my lock had been a gun,
> I'd shoot the blacksmith, for I'm undone,
> And wares to carry I now have none,
> That I should go to Strawberry Fair.

The majority of the most popular folk songs are concerned with love and courtship. But many other matters occupied the attention of the communities which once knew and sang these songs as eagerly as their descendants read the newspapers and listen to the radio. There are songs about war, adventures by sea, wonders and marvels, the trials of domestic life, illegal sports such as poaching and cock-fighting, crime, and the misdemeanours of lawyers and parsons. A perennially favourite topic is the exploits

of popular heroes such as highwaymen, military or naval com-
manders, and the half legendary pioneers of American expansion,
such as John Henry and Casey Jones. All nations have their folk
heroes. Medieval England had its Robin Hood, Australia had the
anonymous swagman celebrated in *Waltzing Matilda*, and the
eighteenth-century sailors sang of the simple manliness and
courage of Admiral Benbow.

> Come all you seamen bold and draw near, and draw near,
> Come all you seamen bold and draw near.
> It's of an Admiral's fame, and brave Benbow was his name,
> How he fought all on the main you shall hear, you shall hear.
>
> Brave Benbow he set sail for to fight, for to fight,
> Brave Benbow he set sail for to fight;
> Brave Benbow he set sail with a fine and pleasant gale,
> But his captains they turned tail in a fright, in a fright.
>
> Says Kirby unto Wade, 'We will run, we will run',
> Says Kirby unto Wade, 'We will run:
> For I value no disgrace, or the losing of my place,
> But the enemy I won't face, nor his guns, nor his guns.'
>
> The Ruby and Benbow fought the French, fought the French,
> The Ruby and Benbow fought the French;
> They fought them up and down till the blood came trickling down,
> Till the blood came trickling down, where they lay, where they lay.
>
> Brave Benbow lost his legs by chain-shot, by chain-shot,
> Brave Benbow lost his legs by chain-shot:
> Brave Benbow lost his legs, and all on his stumps he begs,
> 'Fight on, my English lads, 'tis our lot, 'tis our lot.'
>
> The surgeon dressed his wounds; cries Benbow, cries Benbow:
> The surgeon dressed his wounds; cries Benbow:
> 'Let a cradle now in haste on the quarter-deck be placed,
> That the enemy I may face till I die, till I die.'

Even the arch enemy, Napoleon Bonaparte, was sung of by
British sailors with something like affection:

> Boney was a warrior,
> Way, ay, yah!
> Boney was a warrior,
> John Frans-wah!

This, with its long-drawn-out chorus lines, is one of a class of songs belonging to a limited period in history, the period of the great trading clippers, the late eighteenth to the middle of the nineteenth century. These chanteys, or shanteys, as they were called, achieved considerable variety within a fairly fixed framework. A singer or shantey-man sang or improvised words, and the other seamen, engaged on the rhythmical labours of the ship, joined in a repetitive chorus. Both words and tunes attained, at their best, great heights of beauty and pathos.

> Oh Shenandoah, I'm bound to leave you,
> Away, you rolling river.
> Oh Shenandoah, I'm bound to leave you,
> Away I'm bound to go
> 'Cross the wide Missouri.

Shanteys like *Shenandoah* and *A Yankee Ship* and *Stormalong* reveal depths of poetic feeling and power of expression among ordinary people which it is hard to credit in our days of commercialized mass entertainment. When you think of the stuff poured out day and night by pop stars mouthing the latest Tin Pan Alley concoctions, you may wonder what has become of the unnamed talent, the downright genius which invented the folk songs of yesterday. One of the main features in the change that has come over popular song is of course the commercialization of syncopated negro rhythms and the words that accompany them. So far as the words of the songs are concerned, the negroes of nineteenth-century America made a significant contribution with their religious songs. These 'spirituals', based on popular biblical subjects, are true folk songs, usually direct and vigorous in style, simple in feeling, and often of great imaginative appeal. *Swing Low, Sweet Chariot* and *Deep River* are among the best, and in others there is a fund of humour and shrewd, homely morality. Subjects such as the battle of Jericho and the vision of Ezekiel had a peculiar fascination for the negro mind, while the liberation of the Hebrews from slavery aroused some anonymous singer to utterance of an almost brutal power and directness.

> Go down, Moses,
> Way down in Egypt land,

Tell ole Pharaoh
To let my people go.

It is not possible to illustrate all the variety and richness of our folk-song inheritance, an inheritance which it would be wrong to regard simply as the contents of a museum. What strikes a student most is its uncrushable life and vigour, its sheer force and vitality. Folk songs of a kind are still being written, and inasmuch as the writers are not professional poets, their work may be considered a genuine contribution to folklore—at any rate if it achieves any wide popularity or permanence. But even the work of professional poets, though it may not outwardly resemble a folk song or a ballad, can draw strength and inspiration from the popular anonymous poetry of the past. Whenever a nation's poetry gets too far away from the anonymous culture of its past, it is liable to wilt or wither from over-sophistication and refinement. This was what the poets of the later eighteenth century in England found happening; and the strength which Burns, Blake, Wordsworth and Coleridge drew from the rediscovery of popular balladry gave impetus for a complete poetic revolution.

To sum up—what are the characteristics of the best folk poetry? For what qualities do we value it, even though there seems little chance of adding very much to it? First, it has genuine simplicity. Without being subtle or refined in form, it appeals directly to the common man or woman in each of us. It deals as a rule in subjects of universal interest, not in the odd or eccentric. It expresses true feeling, without sentimentality or sensationalism. It is often the direct expression of love, sorrow, admiration or joy.

In form it is memorable, owing much to repetition and the use of standard turns of phrase; it is essentially a form of oral culture, retained not in books, but in the minds and hearts of ordinary people. In rhythm it exhibits vigour and vitality; it sings itself to melodies equally old and appealing.

Last, and perhaps most important, folk song is often the expression of the spirit of rebellion and non-acceptance of the repressive standards of respectable society. The hero of a folk song is not the civil servant, the government official, the agent of established order, but the man of individuality, the rebel; the concerns of folk song are not church going, conventional bread-winning and family life, but pioneering, poaching, lawbreaking, struggle, conflict and amoral love-making, with or without deplorable consequences. Folk song springs from the desire of every man and woman for freedom, for the right to a full life, and vital self-expression. It is sometimes forgotten that, throughout English history, the established authority, as expressed in Church and State, tried its hardest to suppress popular song as being destructive of public morality. It was driven from the cottage and the field into the tavern, and children were taught hymns and psalms instead. But it was never stamped out, even though much of it lingered only in the memories of old and humble people until those who cared for its recovery wrote it down. It has not thereby been killed. It has a life of its own, which can be extinguished only with the extinction of the human spirit.

CHAPTER 9

KINDS OF POEM—3
The Epic

No exact definition of the term 'epic' quite covers all those poems to which, at various times, it has been applied. The cinema industry has frequently used it to suggest that the kind of film it calls 'epic' is something on a grand scale; and certainly that meaning may be inferred from the use of the word. An epic is a poem on a grand scale, usually in a good many separate books, concerned with the exploits of some great national hero, historical or legendary. That is a good enough definition to go on with.

Epic poetry will not be considered here in great detail, for one very good reason: there are very few poems written in the English language—some would say none—which can properly be called epic. To read the world's true epics in the original, we would have to know Greek, Latin and Italian—perhaps also Hindi, French, Spanish and Portuguese. Many people have read at least part of the two great Greek epics ascribed to Homer; but of these few have read them in Greek. We cannot here discuss epic at second hand—that is, in translation. A brief summary, however, is necessary.

From the point of view of this book, one thing is important about the epic: it may be taken as a bridge between the anonymous narrative poetry we have been discussing under the heading of ballads and poems written by poets whose names are known. It is not certain that the Greek poet Homer ever existed; or if he did, that he was responsible for the two narrative poems ascribed to him. It is possible, however, that one or more ancient Greek poets, living perhaps in the ninth century b.c., perhaps earlier, collected and retold a number of legends about the siege of Troy by Greek warriors (*The Iliad*) and the subsequent adventures of one of these Greek leaders (*The Odyssey*). These two poems, each of twenty-four books, became the national literature of classical Greece.

They were also regarded, during Roman times and the succeeding centuries, as the model for all national epics written in western Europe. The admiration, even reverence, felt for *The Iliad* and *The Odyssey* can be judged from the fact that they have been translated again and again into all western languages. In England alone every few years brings a new translation. Something of the secret of their unfading attraction is expressed in Matthew Arnold's analysis of the three essential qualities of Homer's poetry: rapidity of action and narration—it never drags but moves swiftly and with inevitability across considerable tracts of time; plainness of thought and language—everything seems natural yet dignified, simple yet without crudity; and nobility—human action, both heroic and cruel, is portrayed with a certain grandeur, a certain universality, yet there is ample observation of human nature and appreciation of ordinary human qualities, such as kindness and compassion, to save the narration from bare and primitive ruggedness. These are two of the earliest of the world's epics, and they are the greatest.

The Roman poet Virgil consciously imitated Homer when, towards the end of the first century B.C., he composed his national epic, *The Aeneid*. This consists of twelve books, and relates the adventures of the Trojan hero Aeneas, reputed in legend to have been the founder of Rome, whose greatness Virgil celebrates. *The Aeneid* has had its admirers and imitators at all times, especially during the Renaissance, but few would ascribe to it the universality of Homer, for all its length and the charm of much of the writing, it lacks something of the simplicity, the nobility and the profound humanity of the Greek epics. It has been far less frequently translated.

The growth of the spirit of nationalism in the countries of western Europe produced most of the epics of the Middle Ages and the Renaissance. In France the exploits of the greatest of Charlemagne's paladins were described with great fire and splendour in the anonymous, somewhat primitive twelfth century *Chanson de Roland.*

In Italy, Dante achieved the height of Catholic poetry in his threefold religious poem, *The Divine Comedy.* Later Ariosto wrote his *Orlando Furioso*, based (like the *Chanson de Roland*) on the legends of Charlemagne, in celebration of medieval chivalry, and Tasso composed his *Gierusalemme Liberata*, based on the Crusades. In Spain *El Cid* told of the great conqueror who had withstood the Moors. The Portuguese poet Camoens wrote *The Lusiads*, a great national epic.

When we come to Britain, consideration of the epic becomes more difficult. We have to admit that the nearest thing to a true national epic was written, not in verse, but in prose. The fifteenth-century writer, Sir Thomas Malory, about whom very little is known, composed his *Morte Darthur*, in which he gathered together several cycles of legends, most of which he claimed to have translated from the French, dealing with the half-legendary Romano-British hero, Arthur, and his knights, Lancelot, Galahad, Tristram and a host of others. The *Morte Darthur* is one of the finest prose narratives, or collections of narratives, in the English language, but it is not an epic in our sense. In the nineteenth century Tennyson versified some of Malory's stories, but the titles of his collection, *Idylls of the King*, indicates that he had no epic intention.

Chaucer's long verse narrative of *Troilus and Criseyde* has something of the character of an epic. It deals with a mythological subject on a heroic scale; but Chaucer was interested, not in heroic action for its own sake, but in the tragi-comic elements in what he interpreted as a story of human, and particularly feminine character. His analysis is extraordinarily subtle, and he anticipated the psychological prose novel by several centuries. But he was not an epic poet.

The first who might claim this title in English (we leave aside the author of the anonymous Anglo-Saxon *Beowulf*) was Edmund Spenser, an Elizabethan poet who adopted the method of presentation of the Italian poet, Ariosto. In *The Faerie Queene* he had the ambitious object of personifying twelve virtues as the heroes of the twelve projected books of his poem. In fact, he only completed six. The task proved too much for him. It was his object, as he explained in a letter to his friend Sir Walter Ralegh, 'to fashion a gentleman or noble person in virtuous and gentle discipline'. The intention of the book, though much of its material was drawn from Arthurian legend, was not so much epic as allegorical. The Queen was at once an idealized representation of Queen Elizabeth and the idea of Glory. As a unified conception, it has to be admitted that *The Faerie Queene* is a failure; but it has never ceased to exercise its peculiar charm on succeeding generations of readers, because of the dream-like atmosphere in which its shadowy characters move, and because of the beauty and melody of its language. When Spenser began to write, English was a comparatively harsh and rugged language, somewhat uncertain in rhythm and movement. Chaucer had been at times one of the most melodious of writers, but his fourteenth-century English was now a language of the past—much of it already obsolete. Spenser, whose model was the mellifluous Italian language, consciously aimed at smoothness of harmony and diction, and here he unquestionably succeeded. For his epic or allegory he invented what has come to be known as the Spenserian stanza, used later by other poets, notably Keats. It consists of nine lines, with a carefully interlocking rhyme-scheme, and the last line is two syllables longer than the preceding ones; this produces a slowing down effect and removes the danger of monotony.

> And forth they pass, with pleasure forward led,
> Joying to hear the birds' sweet harmony,
> Which therein shrouded from the tempest dread,
> Seemed in their song to scorn the cruel sky.
> Much can they praise the trees so straight and high,
> The sailing pine, the cedar proud and tall,
> The vine-prop elm, the poplar never dry,
> The builder oak, sole king of forests all,
> The aspen good for staves, the cypress funeral.

The Faerie Queene is perhaps the nearest thing in English to the true verse epic. Its hero, however, is not any national hero, but rather the personified ideal of an Elizabethan gentleman as perceived at the crucial moment of English national expansion and emerging national consciousness. It has little of Matthew Arnold's epic quality: it is not rapid, but leisurely in movement—this is part of its charm; it cannot be said to be natural in thought or diction—it is charmingly artificial; but it has, at least, a largeness and nobility of conception to be found in few poems of equal length. Spenser was obsessed with the idea of magnanimity; he had a true vision of the good society, and he strove to the limits of his powers to express it in language which should give permanent delight and refreshment. The result is a harmonious collection of linked episodes in which the reader will, in certain moods, delight to browse and wander.

Not long after the death of Spenser, Milton schooled himself, from a very early age, deliberately to compose the great national epic he saw himself as cut out to achieve; he determined to do 'Things unattempted yet in prose or rime', as he himself expressed it. He played with a number of ideas, one of which was to write his epic in Latin, another to base it on an Arthurian theme. In the end he selected the subject of the fall of man. His reasons for deciding on the theme of *Paradise Lost*, finally completed in twelve books, were no doubt complex. But undoubtedly one reason was the failure of the political cause he had espoused. After the collapse of the Cromwellian interregnum and the Restoration of the monarchy in 1660, Milton regarded the national cause as lost. He could not deal sincerely with any epic theme of a political character. Religious poetry was, by this time, established in public favour, and the task which now answered to his ambition was, as he put it, to

> assert Eternal Providence,
> And justify the ways of God to men.

It is fair to say that few read *Paradise Lost* for its theology; indeed, it is not easy to say exactly what Milton was really trying to do. It is a long, and in parts tedious poem, which most read for its incidental splendours and passages of narrative power. Whether we enjoy the luxurious descriptions of Paradise or the grim account of Hell or the dramatic recital of Satan's fall, we are bound to take account of one thing—Milton's language. It is round this that controversy has been carried on for over two centuries. It is Milton's language which has had a more lasting and deep-rooted influence than any other aspect of his poetry.

The most remarkable feat in the composition of *Paradise Lost* is the fact that Milton describes scenes and relates incidents, throughout its whole twelve books, which neither he nor anyone else had actually witnessed. Thus there is a built-in artificiality or unreality which is inherent in the language throughout. We rightly value naturalness, but the language of *Paradise Lost* is of necessity the reverse of natural. Milton deliberately created a style in which to compose his poem—a style intended to be dignified, splendid and declamatory. It was in several senses stiff: it was stiff with Latinisms quite foreign to the spoken English of that day or any other day; it was rhythmically and grammatically stiff, preferring classical to English constructions and word-order. A reader who favours naturalness in verse and who enjoys the rhythms of ordinary speech is bound to find Milton's language forbidding and even repugnant. But it must be admitted that poets with very good ears have gone to almost ecstatic lengths in admiring Milton. Tennyson, who had a fine ear, had no objection to Milton's artificiality, and apostrophized him thus:

> O mighty-mouthed inventor of harmonies,
> O skilled to sing of Time or Eternity,
> God-gifted organ-voice of England,
> Milton, a name to resound for ages;

It must be admitted that Tennyson was here writing an exercise in a classical metre, but his words have the ring of sincerity. A poet does not write like that about another poet merely to show how cleverly he can handle a Latin metre. Here are some lines from Book IX, in which Milton compares his task in writing of the fall of man to those of Homer and Virgil. You will notice that, like Greek and Latin verse, it is unrhymed. It consists of five-foot lines (what are called pentameters), and this *blank verse*, as it is called, is the normal metre of Elizabethan verse drama, by which Milton was much influenced.

> I now must change
> Those notes to tragic; foul distrust, and breach
> Disloyal on the part of Man, revolt,
> And disobedience: on the part of Heaven
> Now alienated, distance and distaste,
> Anger and just rebuke, and judgement given,
> That brought into this world a world of woe,
> Sin and her shadow Death, and Misery
> Death's harbinger: sad task, yet argument
> Not less but more heroic than the wrath

Of stern Achilles on his foe pursued
Thrice fugitive about Troy wall; or rage
Of Turnus for Lavinia disespoused,
Or Neptune's ire or Juno's, that so long
Perplexed the Greek and Cytherea's son;
If answerable style I can obtain
Of my celestial Patroness, who deigns
Her nightly visitation unimplored,
And dictates to me slumbering, or inspires
Easy my unpremeditated verse.

This account of epic is necessarily brief, because, as I said earlier, it is not of primary importance in the history of English poetry. There have been many other long narrative poems, but none of first-rate quality which can truly be called epic. Browning composed many long poems, but none has the necessary heroic character. Crabbe was a narrative poet who would perhaps have been happier as a writer of prose fiction. Arnold's *Sohrab and Rustum* has more of the epic spirit, but it is no more than a single episode. Nor is it likely that any English poet, in the foreseeable future, will even attempt to compose a true epic, if only because the time for such poems in our national history is past. Attempts were made continually both before and after Milton's time, but nobody now reads Cowley's *Davideis* or Sir Lewis Morris's *Epic of Hades*.

So far as America is concerned, some have claimed epic status for Longfellow's *Hiawatha*, because it is concerned with the original inhabitants of the North American continent. But the poem is too slight and lyrical for such a claim to be treated seriously. America's true epic poet, if there is one, is perhaps Walt Whitman. But while we might say that *Leaves of Grass*, as a whole, has something of the epic spirit, individual poems, such as *Memories of President Lincoln* and *Song of Myself* are really extended elegy and lyric, without the thread of continuous action which true epic demands.

After all, it must be admitted that the idea of epic is now an anachronism. We look for something else in poetry than we get from epic, and what it gave originally is now supplied by prose chronicle and narrative. Epic originates in a period long before the development of prose as an art. In the primitive sense it belongs to oral culture; like ballads, epics were originally composed to be known by heart. Those of Virgil, Ariosto, Spenser and Milton are literary epics, meant to be read in the study, not recited in public. Yet all of these were written before we had any prose flexible and eloquent enough for the purpose. Epic, then, so far as the western world is concerned, great as it once was and great as are its finest monuments, is a thing not of the present but of the past.

CHAPTER 10

KINDS OF POEM—4
The Lyric

On seeing yet another chapter headed 'Kinds of Poem', you may be saying: 'To me there is only poetry and not poetry; I had no idea of all these subdivisions. Why don't you try to get closer to what poetry really is—*all* poetry?' To this I can only answer: 'This is what I am doing. I want to get nearer to poetry itself, and this is what I hope to do by the end of the book. But the plain fact is that poetry has not always meant the same to people at different times. You must look at it with an historical eye, or there will be many things that will puzzle you as you read it. All the kinds of poetry I have been describing have predominated at different periods. I am working through all of them in order to arrive at what poetry means to the reader of today.'

All the kinds of poem I have talked about so far have been narrative, with the single exception of folk songs, and many of these have a strong narrative element. We may say, then, that most poetry used either to tell a story or to sing a song. But it has other functions too, and these are the subject of this chapter. I don't want to clutter up this book with a lot of names simply for their own sake. But you will come across—if you have not already done so—poems with titles such as *Elegy to the Memory of an Unfortunate Lady, Elegy on the Death of a Mad Dog, Ode to Evening*, or simply *Ode*, or *Sonnet to the River Otter*. Most of such poems were written in the seventeenth, eighteenth and nineteenth centuries; and although you will still see new poems called 'Elegy' or 'Ode' or 'Sonnet' nowadays, they are very much fewer. The fact is that the poets of today no longer think it worth while to make all these distinctions. They call their poems by such titles as *Sailing to Byzantium, The Hollow Men, The Terraced Valley, Winter Remembered, Mending Wall* or *Fern Hill*. Now it is sensible to think of all these simply as *poems* or, if you wish to distinguish this kind of poem from ballads and other narrative poems, as *lyrics*. Most, if not all, the significant poems of the past hundred years have been of the lyric kind. It has for many years been unfashionable, or at any rate old-fashioned, to use such words as 'Elegy' and 'Ode' in the titles of poems. Laurence Binyon wrote a famous elegy on those who died in World War I, but he called it simply *For the Fallen*. Whitman called his poem about Lincoln *Memories of President Lincoln*, though if he had lived fifty years earlier he might have called it an 'elegy', for this is what the poem is.

So, while it is right to think of most non-narrative poems as lyrical, it is also necessary to know something about the various types of lyrical poetry which were formerly commoner than they are now.

From the time of Milton onwards, many poets wrote what they called 'odes'. The definition of an ode is 'rhymed, or rarely unrhymed, lyric, often in form of an address, usually of exalted style and enthusiastic tone, often in varied or irregular metre, and usually between fifty and two hundred lines long'. Milton's *Ode on the Morning of Christ's Nativity* is a formal religious lyric inspired by the idea of Christmas. His *Lycidas* is a funeral ode, or elegy, on the death of a young poet, Edward King, drowned in the Irish Sea. Milton uses the occasion to express his feelings about this tragic and premature death, as well as his observations on the state of the Church in England, and his thoughts about his own future. Here is the conclusion to this movingly written elegy.

> Ay me! Whilst thee the shores and sounding seas
> Wash far away, where e'er thy bones are hurled,
> Whether beyond the stormy Hebrides,
> Where thou perhaps under the whelming tide
> Visit'st the bottom of the monstrous world;
> Or whether thou to our moist vows denied,
> Sleep'st by the fable of Bellerus old,
> Where the great vision of the guarded Mount
> Looks toward Namancos and Bayona's hold;
> Look homeward Angel now, and melt with ruth;
> And, O ye dolphins, waft the hapless youth.
>   Weep no more, woeful shepherds, weep no more,

For Lycidas your sorrow is not dead,
Sunk though he be beneath the wat'ry floor,
So sinks the day-star in the ocean bed,
And yet anon repairs his drooping head,
And tricks his beams, and with new-spangled ore
Flames in the forehead of the morning sky:
So Lycidas sunk low, but mounted high,
Through the dear might of him that walked the waves
Where other groves and other streams along,
With nectar pure his oozy locks he laves,
And hears the unexpressive nuptial song,
In the blest kingdoms meek of joy and love.
There entertain him all the saints above,
In solemn troops and sweet societies
That sing, and singing in their glory move
And wipe the tears for ever from his eyes.
Now Lycidas the shepherds weep no more;
Henceforth thou art the genius of the shore,
In thy large recompense and shalt be good
To all that wander in that perilous flood.

    Thus sang the uncouth swain to the oaks and rills,
While the still morn went out with sandals grey,
He touched the tender stops of various quills
With eager thought warbling his Doric lay;
And now the sun had stretched out all the hills,
And now was dropped into the western bay;
At last he rose and twitched his mantle blue:
Tomorrow to fresh woods and pastures new.

Gray's *Elegy written in a Country Churchyard* expresses the poet's mood of solemn brooding about the extinction of poor obscure country people. The great period of the ode began with Milton's contemporary, Abraham Cowley, who popularized what he called the Pindaric Ode in English—that is, a poem of some length, usually on a subject of public interest or an abstract quality, written in rhymed stanzas of irregular patterns. Cowley's finest ode—which might just as well have been called an elegy—was written about his friend, William Hervey. This is how it begins:

It was a dismal and a fearful night:
Scarce could the morn drive on the unwilling light,

> When sleep, death's image, left my troubled breast
>   By something liker death possessed.
> My eyes with tears did uncommanded flow,
>   And on my soul hung the dull weight
>   Of some intolerable fate.
> What bell was that? Ah me! too much I know!

The form popularized by Cowley remained a favourite with English poets until the middle of the nineteenth century. When Gray wrote his *Ode on a Distant Prospect of Eton College*, what he really meant, expressed simply, was 'Thoughts about my unhappy life at Eton'. Many years later Thomas Hood humorously echoed Gray's idea by writing an *Ode on a Distant Prospect of Clapham Academy*—a poem which deserves to be better known than it is.

> Ay, that's the very house! I know
> Its ugly windows, ten a-row!
>   Its chimneys in the rear!
> And there's the iron rod so high,
> That drew the thunder from the sky,
>   And turned our table-beer!
>
> There I was birched! there I was bred!
> There like a little Adam fed
>   From Learning's woeful tree!
> The weary tasks I used to con!—
> The hopeless leaves I wept upon!—
>   Most fruitless leaves to me!—

The Romantic poets of the end of the eighteenth and the beginning of the nineteenth century, though they were in many ways revolutionary, and wrote in reaction against Gray and his imitators, were nevertheless conservative in retaining the ode and the elegy as two of the forms in which they wrote much of their best poetry. You have only to think of such titles as *Ode: Intimations of Immortality; Dejection: an Ode; Ode to the West Wind; Ode to a Nightingale;* and *Ode on a Grecian Urn*, to realize the truth of this. Keats in particular, the author of the two last, was conspicuous in creating some of his finest poems in the form of Odes. Here is his *Fragment of an Ode to Maia*, in which his verse can be seen at its most beautiful.

Mother of Hermes! and still youthful Maia!
    May I sing to thee
As thou wast hymnèd on the shores of Baiae?
    Or may I woo thee
In earlier Sicilian? or thy smiles
Seek as they once were sought, in Grecian isles,
By bards who died content on pleasant swards
    Leaving great verse unto a little clan?
O give me their old vigour! and unheard
    Save of the quiet primrose, and the span
    Of heaven, and few ears,
Rounded by thee, my song should die away
    Content as theirs,
Rich in the simple worship of a day.

One reason why these forms remained popular in England for so long is undoubtedly that they derived from Greek and Latin practice, and for centuries the classics held sway in English education as the source of all creative writing in verse. It was not till the end of the Romantic period and the beginning of the Victorian era that the ode and the elegy lost their sway. I don't know whether it is true to say that the poet Laureate Tennyson's *Ode on the Death of the Duke of Wellington* was the last considerable ode which anyone remembers. Certainly it was pompous and solemn enough to be a monument to all the odes ever written, and under its weight the form pretty well died a belated death. After the middle of the nineteenth century, though occasional odes continued to be written, the form was definitely regarded as old-fashioned, and any poet who composed one was cultivating something of the atmosphere of a museum. It was the same with the formal elegy.

In thus gradually and almost unconsciously throwing off the influence of Greek and Latin poetry, our poets established what can now be seen as the true and final type of English poetry—the lyric. But of course the true lyric quality had all along been present, whether in odes and elegies, or in songs and other slighter pieces. The ballad and the epic are poems of action; the ode and the elegy, whatever other elements they contain, are essentially formal addresses on public, abstract or impersonal subjects. But the true quality of the lyric is to be *personal*—the vehicle of mood and feeling, the means of exploring the individual sensibility. Lyric poetry is not, of course, a modern invention. It has existed, at least in embryo, for hundreds of years. You can find lyric passages in Chaucer, Skelton, Wyatt—dozens of poets of the sixteenth, fifteenth, and even earlier centuries. But it is not till the later nineteenth century that it established itself as the norm, the accepted type of English poetry. There are many reasons for this, of which perhaps the most important is that we look to prose forms to do almost everything else we want to do with words. Chaucer, Crabbe and Browning all wrote what are essentially novels in verse; even as late as the twentieth century American poets such as Edward Arlington Robinson and Robinson Jeffers, and English poets such as John Masefield, wrote long narratives in verse. But at last it has come to be recognized, perhaps finally, that novel-writing is best done in prose. Even the late Robert Frost wrote tales in verse, but we read them less for the story than for the mood and feeling of the poem. This is not to say that narrative poetry is dead, but we can say that it is no longer expected of a major poet, as it was in Victorian England, to write stories in verse.

The function of poetry in our time has thus come to be expressed in what is generally called the lyric. This is not an altogether happy term, because the word suggests a song, and there is in many modern lyrics very little that is song-like. So we shall have to re-define the word for our own purposes as 'a short poem in no fixed form, expressing a single thought, mood or feeling'. This will cover most of the significant poetry of our time. Every term in the definition is variable, and we cannot look for precision: when we say 'short', for instance, we mean, rather, 'unified', apprehensible as a single train of thought, not extended like a narrative. A lyric may extend from a mere four lines to several pages, but the normal length of a modern lyric is usually from half a page to about two pages. The idea of unity—unity of mood, feeling, thought and style—is also essential to the lyric, which has little room for digressions or looseness of connection. Within these limits a modern poet feels he can accomplish almost everything that poetry can do, say everything that a poem ought to say.

Within these limits, moreover, every variety of form and theme, mood and emotion is possible. Inside the loose and broadly defined compass of the lyric, a poet can achieve all he wishes to of what was once achieved in the ballad, the song, the ode and the elegy.

Before exploring the possibilities of the lyric in greater detail, it remains to say something about one special form which has so far not been discussed, but which is bound to come up in the study of English poetry at almost any time during the past four hundred years. I don't want to treat the sonnet as if it were altogether a thing apart, nevertheless it has to be looked upon as a specialized, the most highly specialized, form of the lyric. For a detailed and technical account of the sonnet you must go to a textbook of poetic forms; all we need to know about it here is that it consists of fourteen pentameters (e.g. 'Shall I compare thee to a summer's day?') arranged either as three rhymed four-line sections (or quatrains) followed by a final rhymed couplet (the Elizabethan or Shakespearean form), or as an octet (eight pentameters with one of several possible rhyme-schemes) followed by a sestet (six pentameters) also with its own special rhyme-scheme (the Miltonic form). The latter form has prevailed from the time of Milton onwards, because the final couplet at the close of the Shakespearean form, in inferior hands, gave an air of artificiality which poets came to dislike. Both forms of the sonnet, however, are highly artificial, and this is one reason why so many poets have been attracted by it. Unlike those poetic forms we got from Latin and Greek, and those of native British origin, the sonnet came from Italy, and the Italian language, unlike English, is rich in rhymes. To find enough rhymes in English, and to express the thought of the sonnet in fourteen pentameters without either padding or excessive compression, was a task which taxed the skill of the most accomplished poet. He regarded it as a challenge. At the same time, the sonnet form provided the relief of offering a fixed pattern in which to work, and this gave a valuable discipline not found in other forms. To write a good sonnet was a severe test of skill. An Elizabethan gentleman was expected to be able to turn out a sonnet, even if not always an inspired one, as one of his normal accomplishments. With only a few notable exceptions, most of the best of the poets from Shakespeare onwards tried their hand at the sonnet, and many succeeded in achieving at least one or two fine examples. The sonnet went entirely out of favour only for comparatively short periods in the late seventeenth and the early and later eighteenth centuries. It is not in high favour at present, but it has not altogether fallen into disuse.

The sonnet is one of the earliest forms in which true lyric feeling is the chief constituent. For the sonnet is, above all, a vehicle for personal emotion. Most Elizabethan sonnets are, indeed, concerned exclusively with love. No doubt the sonnet was felt to be appropriate to the passion of love because its very difficulty would act as a disciplinary influence on what might otherwise run away with the poet. If a young man was afflicted by excessive passion, writing a series of sonnets might do much to cure him. Among the one hundred and fifty-four sonnets of Shakespeare there are many which have never been equalled in intensity, and it is perhaps the prestige attaching to these sonnets which has recommended this form to the poets of later generations. Shakespeare's sonnets need not be quoted here: they should be read in their entirety and with close critical attention. A far less favoured and less esteemed poet, Hartley Coleridge, made the sonnet his best form of expression; and at least one responsible modern critic regarded him as second only to Shakespeare in his handling of the form. We find little perhaps of Shakespeare's intensity of passion or power of intellect, but certainly Hartley Coleridge was able to show considerable mastery in moulding his thoughts and feelings to this most exacting pattern. He is unduly neglected, but the best of his sonnets will assuredly live. Is not such a poem as this worthy to be remembered?

> If I have sinned in act, I may repent;
> If I have erred in thought, I may disclaim
> My silent error, and yet feel no shame—
> But if my soul, big with an ill intent,
> Guilty in will, by fate be innocent,
> Or being bad, yet murmurs at the curse
> And incapacity of being worse
> That makes my hungry passion still keep Lent
> In keen expectance of a Carnival;

Where, in all worlds, that round the sun revolve
And shed their influence on this passive ball,
Abides a power that can my soul absolve?
Could any sin survive, and be forgiven—
One sinful wish would make a hell of heaven.

CHAPTER 11

VARIETIES OF THE LYRIC—1

The end of the previous chapter brought us to the consideration of the lyric as the type of all modern poetry. When we speak of poetry today, as compared with, say, music or painting, we tend to equate the term with 'lyric poetry'. Most of the poems which appear in magazines and anthologies of contemporary verse are lyrics. These are as various as the men and women who write them, as various as all their moods, thoughts and feelings. So, in order to appreciate modern poetry, it is necessary to have some notion of the variety of the lyric. Later we shall explore what is called the technique of verse, because it is interesting in itself and has always been of interest to poets; but an understanding of poetic technique is not necessary to an appreciation of poetry. Nor has much of our best poetry been composed according to fixed rules. Poets, in the old Latin saying, are born, not made; certainly, if they are made, they are self-made. Each poet has to learn his trade for himself, adapting the discoveries of others to his own needs, and making new discoveries of his own. So that we have to admit that, while every poet's technique may be important to himself, it is not very important to the reader. It follows, then, that to classify poems into sonnets, ballads, odes and so on, though it may help us to keep our ideas about poetry orderly, helps little in the formation of a love of poetry. Only poems themselves can do this.

Every good poem has a life of its own, its peculiar atmosphere, flavour, emotional key. The appreciation of one poem does not help us much in the appreciation of others, except to foster a general taste for poetry and a desire for more. The only way to acquire a love of poetry is to read poems, rejecting those that mean little to us, re-reading and remembering those that have some peculiar attraction for us. I may write about poems in chapter after chapter; but in the end the best, perhaps the only thing I can do is to point out some of the poems which have moved and still move me deeply. For I believe it is the business of a poem to move the reader: this may not be its primary purpose for the poet, but it is the ground of its survival for the reading public. Some mentally ill people make private communications to themselves, which presumably afford them pleasure or relief; but if such communications are sheer nonsense, they can mean nothing to a reader. However different, however individual the poet is, the value of his work lies in its use of a language common to him and the rest of the world, at any rate the educated world. I shall take a number of poems that mean something to me, and discuss them without going into great detail; for, however clever the literary critics are, a poem has to make its own impact; if you have followed me so far, I think you will be able to accept or reject these poems, even if you cannot say exactly why. Remember that it was a very great poet, Samuel Taylor Coleridge, who said that poetry is at its best when only imperfectly understood. This is not to say it is incomprehensible; it means that poetry achieves its effect partly through non-intellectual means. Magic is not magic if it can be wholly explained. I would be the last to say *why* these poems are to me moving; I can only be sure that, after many readings, they still are.

The sonnet by Hartley Coleridge which I quoted at the end of the previous chapter is concerned with guilt. The poet was expressing, and thereby finding relief from, a feeling of profound self-reproach. This is something which many of us have felt, and poets have often expressed. They express it in quite different ways. This is how A. E. Housman treats the theme. His poem is very different from Hartley Coleridge's.

> Others, I am not the first,
> Have willed more mischief than they durst:
> If in the breathless night I too
> Shiver now, 'tis nothing new.
>
> More than I, if truth were told,
> Have stood and sweated hot and cold,
> And through their reins in ice and fire
> Fear contended with desire.

Agued once like me were they,
But I like them shall win my way
Lastly to the bed of mould
Where there's neither heat nor cold.

But from my grave across my brow
Plays no wind of healing now,
And fire and ice within me fight
Beneath the suffocating night.

The shorter lines, rhymed in pairs, at once give this poem a
sense of urgency, of unusual intensity. The rhythm is measured
and regular, expressing the mood of deliberate and remorseless
self-accusation. Housman begins by identifying himself with all
those who have suffered from a sense of guilt, a guilt which can
only end in the grave. But what isolates Housman from these
others is the fact that he still lives and suffers. There is no hysteria
or over-statement, nothing but a stoical and sardonic admission
of the awfulness of his situation. Neither is there any self-pity, and
this is perhaps the reason why our compassion is wrung from us.
We can imagine how much it cost Housman to write the poem.
Such an effect cannot be faked. Is it too much to say that part of
the power of the poem comes to us directly from the suffering it
has cost the poet?

For another poem of self-exploration, let us return to Hartley
Coleridge.

Long time a child, and still a child, when years
Had painted manhood on my cheek, was I—
For yet I live like one not born to die;
A thriftless prodigal of smiles and tears,
No hope I needed, and I knew no fears.
But sleep, though sweet, is only sleep, and waking,
I waked to sleep no more, at once o'ertaking
The vanguard of my age, with all arrears
Of duty on my back. Nor child, nor man,
Nor youth, nor sage, I find my head is grey,
For I have lost the race I never ran:
A rathe December blights my lagging May;
And still I am a child, tho' I be old,
Time is my debtor for my years untold.

Like Housman's poem, this too demands our compassion. The poet does not wallow in self-pity, but calmly dissects the course of his unfulfilled life. There is no nocturnal agony, but rather a pathetic statement of a sense of futility, not less deeply, though perhaps less passionately, experienced. Even if we did not know of the literal truth of Hartley Coleridge's summing-up of his life, we could not doubt the sincerity of his admission: 'I have lost the race I never ran'.

We might say that this poet was prematurely old, his hair grey before its time. He lived in fact for less than fifty-three years. Thomas Hardy, born only a few years before Hartley Coleridge's death, lived to a great age, and he, like other ageing poets, ruminated often on the effects of growing old.

> I look into my glass,
> And view my wasting skin,
> And say, 'Would God it came to pass
> My heart had shrunk as thin!'
>
> For then I, undistrest
> By hearts grown cold to me,
> Could lonely wait my endless rest
> With equanimity.
>
> But Time, to make me grieve,
> Part steals, lets part abide;
> And shakes this fragile frame at eve
> With throbbings of noontide.

It is sure evidence of the magic of a poem that one is never absolutely certain that one has quite understood it. This seems clear and simple enough. But what exactly is Hardy's mood? Is it one of self-pity? For this is an emotion for which we do not ordinarily respect people. But beneath the apparently direct statement of self-pity there is a note of irony typical of Hardy. For what he is saying in the last stanza is that, as an old man, he is afflicted by the same passionate sensibility as he felt in the prime of life. He wishes, he says in the first stanza, that his heart were as withered and shrunken as his body. But we are not intended to take this literally, and we do not take it so. There is, in fact, an underlying note of quiet and dignified pride in having retained the sensitivity of youth and not become hard, even though being alive in this way inevitably causes some pain. What we admire in the mood and tone of the poem is its calm, dignified refusal to be comforted by illusions.

I quote now a strange poem, very different from Hardy's. It is *Tea at the Palaz of Hoon* by the American poet, Wallace Stevens. I must say at once that I don't fully understand it, though it retains for me a mysterious and moving quality.

> Not less because in purple I descended
> The western day through what you called
> The loneliest air, not less was I myself.
>
> What was the ointment sprinkled on my beard?
> What were the hymns that buzzed beside my ears?
> What was the sea whose tide swept through me there?
>
> Out of my mind the golden ointment rained,
> And my ears made the blowing hymns they heard.
> I was myself the compass of that sea:
>
> I was the world in which I walked, and what I saw
> Or heard or felt came not but from myself;
> And there I found myself more truly and more strange.

Look first at the final line, 'And there I found myself more truly and more strange'. This gives the clue to the meaning. It is a poem about self-discovery, one of the primary themes of much modern poetry. Stevens begins by imagining himself as a sort of purple-robed eastern emperor enjoying great acclaim, and inspired, perhaps to prophetic utterance, by a sea of inspiration which surges through him. But all the acclaim and the inspiration was self-engendered. Yet he was none the less himself, though he felt himself isolated from the common world. Through experiencing the loneliness of the creative artist, something of a pioneer in twentieth-century democratic America, he discovers his real self. This is a far from simple poem, with none of the direct, natural speech of Hardy. It is, in fact, a highly sophisticated essay in self-discovery, and could perhaps only have been written by one who felt himself to be an aristocrat of aesthetic individualism in a democracy of mass culture, and mediocrity. All poets are at times taken up, directly or indirectly, with being different from the rest of society, and American poets are especially preoccupied with this problem. A poet is, almost by definition, an individualist; he stands for the private, as distinct from the public values, and for the protection of private sensibility against the influence of the mass. This is not because he despises the mass; on the contrary, he tries to see the mass as individuals like himself, equally able to cultivate their separateness.

An earlier American poet, Emily Dickinson, developed an almost obsessive concern for her own separateness. She was the most original poet of her time, living in virtually complete isolation from her fellow-creatures during the second half of her life. Only by withdrawing could she discover herself. Yet there was nothing egocentric in her self-cultivation. She left the world in order to be able to understand it and value it justly. Her observation was acute, and her power of selecting significant details remarkable. She was intensely interested in the phenomenon of loneliness, and in this poem she allows her imagination to play with the idea of burgling some isolated house in the country.

> I know some lonely houses off the road
> A robber'd like the look of,—
> Wooden barred,
> And windows hanging low,
> Inviting to
> A portico,
> Where two could creep:
> One hand the tools,
> The other peep
> To make sure all's asleep.
> Old-fashioned eyes,
> Not easy to surprise!
>
> How orderly the kitchen'd look by night,
> With just a clock,—
> But they could gag the tick,
> And mice won't bark.
> And so the walls don't tell,
> None will.

A pair of spectacles ajar just stir—
An almanack's aware.
Was it the mat winked,
Or a nervous star?
The moon slides down the stair
To see who's there.

There's plunder,—where?
Tankard, or spoon,
Earring, or stone,
A watch, some ancient brooch
To match the grandmamma,
Staid sleeping there.

Day rattles, too,
Stealth's slow;
The sun has got as far
As the third sycamore.
Screams chanticleer,
'Who's there?'
And echoes, trains away,
Sneer—'Where?'
While the old couple, just astir,
Fancy the sunrise left the door ajar.

This extraordinary poem is deceptively simple. Yet you might say that its simplicity, its graphic realism is achieved with consummate art; I would prefer to say that its art is achieved by the poet's personal involvement in the scene. It is not so much that she observes the domestic interior—almanack, spectacles, moonlit stair and the rest—as that she *feels* the physical presence of these things with a total and preternaturally alert consciousness. She does not simply describe the scene, she creates it, and it is unforgettable. It is like a ghost-story with no action, a brief suspense tale achieved with the utmost economy. She notices the scene and imagines a story to be enacted in it. There is something faintly sinister in this unplayed drama. This exploitation of the power of suggestion in ordinary subjects is not the least of Emily Dickinson's special gifts.

For contrast, here is a short poem, *Daydreams*, by William Canton.

Broad August burns in milky skies,
  The world is blanched with hazy heat;
The vast green pastures, even, lies
  Too hot and bright for eyes and feet.

Amid the grassy levels rears
  The sycamore against the sun
The dark boughs of a hundred years,
  The emerald foliage of one.

Lulled in a dream of shade and sheen,
  Within the clement twilight thrown
By that great cloud of floating green,
  A horse is standing, still as stone.

He stirs nor head nor hoof, although
  The grass is fresh beneath the branch;
His tail alone swings to and fro
  In graceful curves from haunch to haunch.

He stands quite lost, indifferent
  To rack or pasture, trace or rein;
He feels the vaguely sweet content
  Of perfect sloth in limb and brain.

This is an unpretentious lyric without great emotional pressure, but with a certain solid charm. It illustrates the fact that even a descriptive poem is seldom purely descriptive. You cannot keep feeling out of poetry, and here the feeling is one of savouring and cherishing the atmosphere of peace and contentment that is evoked. The descriptive function of lyric poetry is not its highest; but poets have always stood for the full realization of the strength to be drawn from a love of the natural scene. The attraction of the poem is achieved by the fastidious care with which the words are chosen, and the rhythmic sense that keeps the lines moving slowly and placidly along.

Andrew Young's *Field-Glasses* is a much more artfully composed poem based on a love of natural life. Here the poet is enjoying, not only his intimate view of the birds, but also his isolation and the privacy which his field-glasses confer upon him.

Though buds still speak in hints
And frozen ground has set the flints

As fast as precious stones
And birds perch on the boughs, silent as cones,

Suddenly waked from sloth
Young trees put on a ten years' growth
And stones double their size,
Drawn nearer through field-glasses' greater eyes.

Why I borrow their sight
Is not to give small birds a fright
Creeping up close by inches;
I make the trees come, bringing tits and finches.

I lift a field itself
As lightly as I might a shelf,
And the rooks do not rage
Caught for a moment in my crystal cage.

And while I stand and look,
Their private lives an open book,
I feel so privileged
My shoulders prick, as though they were half-fledged.

There is a sort of cool detachment about many of Young's brief poems which makes them unique. In them the intellectual elements of thought and speculation finely balance the sensuous elements of a naturalist's pure observation. He observes with detachment, but is always intensely interested in his own reactions to what he notes. There is always this combination of the recording eye and the speculating mind.

I have used the expression 'cool passion' of Young's poem. It might be applied also to this, by Dante Gabriel Rossetti, entitled *The Woodspurge*.

The wind flapped loose, the wind was still,
Shaken out dead from tree and hill.
I had walked on at the wind's will,—
I sat now, for the wind was still.

Between my knees my forehead was,—
My lips, drawn in, said not Alas!
My hair was over in the grass,
My naked ears heard the day pass.

G

My eyes, wide open, had the run
Of some ten weeds to fix upon;
Among these few, out of the sun,
The woodspurge flowered, three cups in one.

From perfect grief there need not be
Wisdom or even memory:
One thing then learnt remains to me,—
The woodspurge has a cup of three.

Again, I don't know quite how to express the extraordinary
fascination of this poem, apparently so slight, so inconsequential,
yet at the same time so surprising, so uncommon in its faithfulness
to what was obviously a genuine and moving experience. We are
told nothing of the 'grief' by which the poet was overcome; but
we are convinced of its seriousness and power by the clarity with
which the poet retains the unusual, almost trivial picture which
the intensity of his grief impressed on his mind. We are reminded
that Rossetti was also a painter, but this is not enough to account
for the rare truth of feeling in this poem.

The varieties of lyric poetry are infinite. In every good lyric
there is something unique. What we look for is its strangeness,
its newness, and at the same time its truth: we recognize it as
something we had previously guessed at, at least in part. This is
one of those paradoxes we are always coming up against in
thinking about poetry. When we have read a poem of the highest
quality for the first time, we think, 'How true—how natural' and
simultaneously 'How new—how unexpected.' Moreover, this
happens, not simply the first time we read it, but every time. I
have read over and over again Walter De la Mare's *The Railway
Junction* without ever being quite sure what it means, but with an
increasing sense of the power of suggestion it holds.

From here through tunnelled gloom the track
Forks into two; and one of these
Wheels onward into darkening hills,
And one toward distant seas.

How still it is; the signal light
At set of sun shines palely green;
A thrush sings; other sound there's none,
Nor traveller to be seen—

Where late there was a throng. And now,
In peace awhile, I sit alone;
Though soon, at the appointed hour,
I shall myself be gone.

But not their way: the bow-legged groom,
The parson in black, the widow and son,
The sailor with his cage, the gaunt
Gamekeeper with his gun,

That fair one, too, discreetly veiled—
All, who so mutely came, and went,
Will reach those far nocturnal hills,
Or shores, ere night is spent.

I nothing know why thus we met—
Their thoughts, their longings, hopes, their fate:
And what shall I remember, except—
The evening growing late—

That here through tunnelled gloom the track
Forks into two; of these
One into darkening hills leads on,
And one toward distant seas?

A company of strangers has just departed by train, leaving the
junction deserted except for the poet. They are on their way either
to the hills or to the sea; the poet is soon to depart in yet a third,
unspecified direction. The company was an odd but strangely
significant cross-section—a servant, a clergyman, a widow with
her son, a sailor, a gamekeeper and a mysterious woman, anxious
not to be recognized. 'I nothing know why thus we met' is the
poet's comment after they have gone. It is late in the evening, and
he himself must soon depart also, but to another destination. It
would be easy to read into this an allegory of human life, but
perhaps this would be wrong. The experience itself, despite the
mystery which surrounds it, is vivid and concrete enough; possibly
the poet did not want to explain it too precisely. All one can be
sure of is that one element in the poem is a sense of the loneliness
of the human situation. Perhaps even the strange company were
strangers to each other. The poet is in no doubt as to his own
isolation. To me there is something curiously compelling about

this poem. I am convinced there is more in it that I have discovered, and I want to know what it is. The poem seems to me to
imply that life is by no means without significance, but that we
don't know just what that significance is.

CHAPTER 12

VARIETIES OF THE LYRIC—2

The difficulty in thinking about the varieties of lyric poetry is that they are virtually infinite—or at least as infinite as the varieties of mood and feeling to be experienced by human beings. One of the pleasures arising from a knowledge of lyric poetry is that it gives the reader scope for contemplating the expression of one mood by one poet, another by another, a feeling expressed in this way by one poet, in that way by another. There is no form of art or expression which gives wider range to our thoughts and feelings. Consider, for instance, the emotion of love. There is a sense in which all love is the same—a compound of admiration, desire, and the wish to serve. But the varieties of love, as expressed in all the human relationships that can be named by this word, are infinite. So too are the varieties of lyric poetry inspired by love. It would need at least a book to describe all these varieties. I shall quote only one love poem, somewhat different in style and expression from the other lyrics here considered. Here is *The Fair Singer* by Andrew Marvell.

> To make a final conquest of all me,
> Love did compose so sweet an enemy,
> In whom both beauties to my death agree,
> Joining themselves in fatal harmony;
> That while she with her eyes my heart does bind,
> She with her voice might captivate my mind.
>
> I could have fled from one but singly fair:
> My disentangled soul itself might save,
> Breaking the curlèd trammels of her hair.
> But how should I avoid to be her slave,
> Whose subtle art invisibly can wreathe
> My fetters of the very air I breathe?
>
> It had been easy fighting in some plain,
> Where victory might hang in equal choice.
> But all resistance against her is vain

> Who has th'advantage both of eyes and voice.
> And all my forces needs must be undone,
> She having gainèd both the wind and sun.

To a reader accustomed to modern speech this poem will at first seem strange. Andrew Marvell was a seventeenth-century poet, and he uses the style and language of two hundred years ago. No one would dream of writing a love poem like this nowadays. It seems exceedingly artificial; yet who could say that it is insincere? The thought that strikes the poet as he gazes at a beautiful girl while she sings is that she captivates him in two quite different ways—by the power of sight and the power of sound. He imagines her effect on him to be like a military conquest, and he is overcome on two fronts. The beauty both of her appearance and her voice is reflected in the grave and tranquil beauty of the language, in the note of serious and restrained passion to be heard in the rhythm. Of course this is an intellectual kind of poetry, with a faint undertone of humour, the reverse of spontaneous, uncontrolled passion as expressed in some love poems. The poet works out in his mind the idea which his senses have suggested to him. Notice, too, the conceit, as it is called, in the last line—'She having gained both the wind and sun'. The advantages which a military commander would get from having both wind and sun in his favour are gained by the singer from the combined effect of her voice (the wind) and her beauty (the sun).

I would like next to consider a poem as fully contrasted with this one as it is possible to imagine. Yet it too is in a sense an expression of love. Walt Whitman was actuated in much of his *Leaves of Grass* by a large-hearted, almost indiscriminate love of his fellow-men. Where Marvell is particular and fastidious, Whitman is general and all-embracing. He often addresses large sections of humanity, rather than one particular person. You would expect his style to be the very opposite of Marvell's, and it is. He seems almost deliberately careless, using the rhythms, not of formal verse, but of speech. His vocabulary is well chosen, but you would hardly call it carefully chosen.

> You felons on trial in courts,
> You convicts in prison-cells, you sentenced assassins

Chained and hand-cuffed with iron,
Who am I too that I am not on trial or in prison?
Me, ruthless and devilish as any, that my wrists are not chained with
    iron, or my ankles with iron?

You prostitutes flaunting over the trottoirs or obscene in your rooms,
Who am I that I should call you more obscene than myself?
O culpable! I acknowledge—I exposé!
(O admirers, praise not me—compliment not me—you make me
    wince,
I see what you do not—I know what you do not.)
Inside these breast-bones I lie smutched and choked,
Beneath this face that appears so impassive hell's tides continually run,
Lusts and wickedness are acceptable to me,
I walk with delinquents with passionate love,
I feel I am of them—I belong to those convicts and prostitutes myself,
And henceforth I will not deny them—for how can I deny myself?

Here we have something that was quite new in lyric poetry. It
is a passionate manifesto announcing a sense of community with
the most despised of humanity. Formal rhythm and contrived
rhyme would have been out of place in anything so immediate
and novel. Whitman does not sentimentalize over criminals and
evil-doers, he goes further, identifying himself with them, even
going so far as to say that to deny such people was to deny himself: he recognizes the streak of potential criminality in all of us.
Underlying Whitman's outburst is an implied criticism of the
respectable society in which he found himself in mid-nineteenth-
century America. At other times he felt something like despair.
Here is another short poem, entitled *The Beasts*, in which he
attacks human society, by implication, for its respectability, its
self-pity, its reverence for the past.

I think I could turn and live with animals, they are so placid and self-
    contained;
I stand and look at them long and long.
They do not sweat and whine about their condition;
They do not lie awake in the dark and weep for their sins;
They do not make me sick discussing their duty to God;
Not one is dissatisfied—not one is demented with the mania of owning
things;

Not one kneels to another, nor to his kind that lived thousands of
    years ago;
Not one is respectable and industrious over the whole earth.

This is a very arresting idea, struck out of the poet's mind
almost like a crude sculpture struck from the living rock at one
blow. It has taken a long time for the kind of free verse practised
by Whitman to be accepted as a legitimate poetic form. It must
always be a matter of debate as to whether poems gain or lose by
such informality. Whitman is anxious to give the impression of
immediacy, urgency and spontaneity to his poems, as if he felt that
to work them into an accepted form would subtract from these
qualities. Whitman's free verse was absolutely characteristic of
the man, and we cannot conceive of his ever having written much
in any other form. It must be admitted that very few poets have
managed to make it their own.

The nineteenth century, in which Whitman wrote, was an
age when middle-class industriousness and smug respectability
amounted almost to a tyranny. A poet, while essentially he feels,
as Whitman did, one with all humanity, must also sometimes feel
alone. A poet is a pioneer of feeling, and all pioneers suffer at
times from a sense of isolation. Here is another expression of the
same idea by another nineteenth-century American, Jones Very.
It is called *The Strangers*.

> Each care-worn face is but a book
>   To tell of houses bought or sold;
> Or filled with words that mankind took
>   From those who lived and spoke of old.
>
> I see none whom I know, for they
>   See other things than him they meet;
> And though they stop me by the way,
>   'Tis still some other one to greet.
>
> There are no words that reach my ear
>   Those speak who tell of other things
> Than what they mean for me to hear,
>   For in their speech the counter rings.
>
> I would be where each word is true,
>   Each eye sees what it looks upon;

> For here my eye has seen but few,
> Who in each act that act have done.

In form this is a complete contrast to Whitman; but the attitude is very close to his. Jones Very expresses himself quietly, gravely, almost under-emphatically. Yet is he the less effective? He is protesting against the commercialism around him. He is also saying that he, the poet, yearns for a more natural and truthful state of society, where people are sincere and enjoy the sense of reality which a true relation with other people brings. Both Jones Very and Whitman criticize society, but they do so from the standpoint of two contrasted temperaments. You may prefer one or the other, according to your own temperament; it would be hard to say which is the better poem, *The Beasts* or *The Strangers*. I believe that opinion would be pretty equally divided. The point I want to make, however, is that it is not necessary to prefer one poem to the other. It is better to be able to respond to each sympathetically and with understanding.

Arthur Hugh Clough was an English contemporary of Whitman and Very, and he too was oppressed by the insincerity, the humbug engendered by Victorian values—respectability, materialism and an outward show of godliness. His protest was the more effective for being expressed as a parody of the ten commandments.

> Thou shalt have one God only; who
> Would be at the expense of two?
>
> No graven images may be
> Worshipped, except the currency:
>
> Swear not at all; for, for thy curse
> Thine enemy is none the worse:
>
> At church on Sunday to attend
> Will serve to keep the world thy friend:
>
> Honour thy parents; that is, all
> From whom advancement may befall:
>
> Thou shalt not kill; but need'st not strive
> Officiously to keep alive:

Do not adultery commit;
Advantage rarely comes of it:

Thou shalt not steal; an empty feat,
When 'tis so lucrative to cheat:

Bear not false witness; let the lie
Have time on its own wings to fly:

Thou shalt not covet, but tradition
Approves all forms of competition.

It is now common to satirize the middle-class virtues, but in Clough's day it needed a certain courage to express oneself like this. Social satire was perfectly in order by the end of the century, and the generation of Bernard Shaw made a business of attacking all established values. But Clough, writing in the very middle of the century, was a pioneer.

It is interesting to notice how often satire takes the form of parody or imitation. This is not perhaps a very exalted form of poetry. It is too easy, and requires little originality. It is, as has been said, a form in which mediocrity can excel. Nevertheless, in a few instances, such as the one just quoted, a parody or imitation may have the force of something original. Samuel Butler's *Psalm of Montreal* relies for its fun on the imitation of Anglican psalmody, while losing nothing of its effectiveness as an expression of Butler's sense of despondency on meeting with prudish respectability in Canada. It is a good-humoured attack on people who thought it shameful to exhibit nude classical sculpture. It is more than that: it is a piece of ridicule against the subordination of art to middle-class ideals.

Stowed away in a Montreal lumber room
The Discobolus standeth and turneth his face to the wall;
Dusty, cobweb-covered, maimed and set at nought,
Beauty lieth in an attic and no man regardeth:
O God! O Montreal!

Beautiful by night and day, beautiful in summer and winter,
Whole or maimed, always and alike beautiful—
He preacheth gospel of grace to the skins of owls
And to one who seasoneth the skins of Canadian owls;
O God! O Montreal!

When I saw him I was wroth and said, 'O Discobolus!
Beautiful Discobolus, a Prince both among Gods and men,
What dost thou here, how camest thou hither, Discobolus,
Preaching gospel in vain to the skins of owls?'
    O God! O Montreal!

And I turned to the man of skins and said unto him, 'O thou man of
    skins,
Wherefore hast thou done thus to shame the beauty of the Disco-
    bolus?'
But the Lord had hardened the heart of the man of skins
And he answered, 'My brother-in-law is haberdasher to Mr Spurgeon.'
    O God! O Montreal!

'The Discobolus is put here because he is vulgar,
He has neither vest nor pants with which to cover his limbs;
I, Sir, am a person of most respectable connections—
My brother-in-law is haberdasher to Mr Spurgeon.'
    O God! O Montreal!

Then I said, 'O brother-in-law to Mr Spurgeon's haberdasher,
Who seasonest also the skins of Canadian owls,
Thou callest trousers "pants", whereas I call them "trousers",
Therefore thou art in hell-fire, and may the Lord pity thee!'
    O God! O Montreal!

'Preferrest thou the gospel of Montreal to the gospel of Hellas,
The gospel of thy connection with Mr Spurgeon's haberdashery to the
    gospel of the Discobolus?'
Yet none the less blasphemed he beauty saying, 'The Discobolus hath
    no gospel,
But my brother-in-law is haberdasher to Mr Spurgeon.'
    O God! O Montreal!

I have stressed throughout these pages on lyric poetry that it
is, above all, the poetry of personal feeling; so long as poets are
individuals, all different from one another, and so long as they
feel impelled to express their feelings in durable form, there will
be lyric poetry. One of the emotions commonest to men at all
times is that of love, and our best lyric poetry is love poetry. But
there is also a poetry of hate, itself often a pure and immediate
emotion. Satire is often engendered by the desire to improve
society, to right a wrong. But the most effective satire will be that

in which some hatred is felt, and the poet wants to work it off.
I have said that Whitman was actuated by a love of mankind; but
he also felt hatred against its stupidity and hypocrisy. An element
of hate is also discernible in the poems I quoted by Clough and
Butler. Here is a pure hate poem, in a sense humorous, but inspired by no desire to reform or alter anything, merely the need
to work off a violent resentment. James Stephens was an Irishman,
and the Irish tradition is rich in invective, since it was believed
that a poetic curse had a magical power to destroy its object. Here
is a poem by James Stephens called *A Glass of Beer*.

> The lanky hank of a she in the inn over there
> Nearly killed me for asking the loan of a glass of beer;
> May the devil grip the whey-faced slut by the hair,
> And beat bad manners out of her skin for a year.
>
> That parboiled ape, with the toughest jaw you will see
> On virtue's path, and a voice that will rasp the dead,
> Came roaring and raging the minute she looked at me,
> And threw me out of the house on the back of my head!
>
> But if I asked her master he'd give me a cask a day;
> But she, with the beer at hand, not a gill would arrange!
> May she marry a ghost and bear him a kitten, and may
> The High King of Glory permit her to get the mange.

No doubt this is half in fun. But there is no humorous intention
in Rossetti's lines *On the Site of a Mulberry-tree planted by William Shakespeare, felled by the Rev. F. Gastrell*, an eighteenth-
century parson.

> This tree, here fall'n, no common birth or death
> Shared with its kind. The world's enfranchised son,
> Who found the trees of Life and Knowledge one,
> Here set it, frailer than his laurel-wreath.
> Shall not the wretch whose hand it fell beneath
> Rank also singly—the supreme unhung?
> Lo! Sheppard, Turpin, pleading with black tongue
> This viler thief's unsuffocated breath!
> We'll search thy glossary, Shakespeare! whence almost,
> And whence alone, some name shall be revealed
> For this deaf drudge, to whom no length of ears
> Sufficed to catch the music of the spheres;

Whose soul is carrion now,—too mean to yield
Some Starveling's ninth allotment of a ghost.

In these lines, it seems to me, Rossetti raises invective to impassioned heights. There have been a number of expressions of intense admiration for the greatest of poets—by Ben Jonson, Milton and Arnold—but none has more conviction and trenchancy than Rossetti's.

I have chosen deliberately to move at random through the manifold varieties of lyric poetry, because a more systematic account would give a false impression. The human temper, its moods and feelings, are wayward and unsystematic, and it is the business of lyric poetry to respond to all the movements and impulses of the mind. I have discussed the sonnet, as well as various lyrical forms, both regular and free, and I have said something about minor forms such as parody and imitation. All have their place in the resources available to poets. I have said little about length, because this is a matter on which little can be said. It is entirely up to the poet, unless he is using a set form such as the sonnet, to determine how long his poem should be; indeed, repeating what I have said before, that every true poem has a life of its own, I would go further and say that a true poem determines its own dimensions. A lyric is usually defined as 'short', and this word is left intentionally vague. We have discussed the ballad and the ode, usually but not always too long to be properly called lyrics. Collins' *Ode: How Sleep the Brave*, a mere twelve lines, is an obvious exception.

A final word, however, should be said about the briefest form of all, the epigram. This may be as short as two lines, indeed the shorter the more effective. Like the parody, the epigram is not usually rated very high; yet it is surprising how few really memorable epigrams there are. The qualities of a good epigram are pithiness, point and neatness of form. You might say that the epigram is the nursery-rhyme of the adult world, often a mere intellectual *jeu d'esprit*.

Faith is a fine invention
When gentlemen can see,
But microscopes are prudent
In an emergency.

So wrote Emily Dickinson commenting on the need to supplement religious faith by scientific investigation. No doubt she was replying to some preacher who had asserted the all-sufficiency of faith; such dogmatism always aroused her opposition.

But an epigram can on occasions be more than a neat and pregnant comment on some person or institution. It might be thought that the economy of form demanded in an epigram would exclude strong emotion: there is usually an element of cleverness in an epigram, and cleverness is apt to inhibit strong feeling. Perhaps it would not be strictly right to call Rossetti's couplet entitled *Memory* an epigram. At all events, it is hard to imagine more emotional force and profound personal experience compressed into two short lines.

> Is Memory most of miseries miserable,
> Or the one flower of ease in bitterest hell?

CHAPTER 13

POETIC TECHNIQUE

Technique is a bad word. It suggests that the writing of poetry is a matter of tricks and gimmicks. But it is the only word that will serve.

So far we have discussed mainly the 'What?' and the 'Why?' of poetry. Now we have to talk about the 'How?' In practice the 'How?' is not, or should not be, separate from the 'Why?' and the 'What?' But we can't discuss all the aspects of poetry simultaneously. We must discuss them separately; but remember—they are inseparable. The 'How?' of poetry—how it is written, how language and form are chosen—is best referred to simply as technique.

I have said that poetry is inspired. But 'technique', you may think, suggests a coldly logical process. What has the heat of inspiration to do with the cool processes of technique? I once gave a lecture on poetic inspiration and said that all good poetry was inspired. Up jumped one of my audience and asked, 'What about a sonnet?' It was a good question. As I have said earlier, a sonnet is an intricate and technically difficult form for any poet. Nevertheless, within its given framework it can be inspired. Of all those who have tried their hand at this form, however, few can be regarded as having been inspired. It is too often a contrived form; inspiration, when it appears, usually shows itself in single lines or phrases—rarely in the whole fourteen lines of a sonnet. Indeed, I am inclined to think that Shakespeare alone maintained his inspiration throughout the whole of a sonnet.

It may be asked, 'Can a poet have inspiration without technique?' or again, 'Can a poet have technique without inspiration?' To take the second question first, since it is the easier, it can readily be seen that technique may exist without inspiration. The result is usually flat, dull and not memorable. To consider in detail many actual examples would be depressing, but let us look at just one.

Father! to God himself we cannot give
A holier name! then lightly do not bear
Both names conjoined, but of thy spiritual care
Be duly mindful: still more sensitive
Do Thou, in truth a second Mother, strive
Against disheartening custom, that by Thee
Watched, and with love and pious industry
Tended at need, the adopted Plant may thrive
For everlasting bloom. Benign and pure
This Ordinance, whether loss it would supply,
Prevent omission, help deficiency,
Or seek to make assurance doubly sure.
Shame if the consecrated Vow be found
An idle form, the Word an empty sound!

This is a sonnet by Wordsworth entitled *Sponsors*, written when the inspiration that had fired his early genius was spent, and he had nothing left but a well-practised command of poetic form —correct rhythm and rhyme, ability to express what he wanted to say in adequate language, command over the standard form of the sonnet or whatever else he was attempting. Many elderly poets find they have this technical facility, which in reality is no more than the capacity to imitate other poets or themselves when in the full tide of their poetic power.

What I said just now about Wordsworth will serve to suggest a definition of technique: it is, briefly, the ability to match the form and language of the poem to the thought and mood which the poet wants to convey. A grasp of poetic form implies the power to create poetic movement through rhythm. It implies also the power to find the right words and images, and this means that a poet, probably though not certainly, possesses a large vocabulary and a large and graphic imagination. All these terms—rhythm, diction, imagery and imagination—we shall consider in detail later. For the moment it will be enough to insist that they constitute the fabric of poetry, and over them the poet must have command.

This brings us to the earlier question, 'Can you have inspiration without technique?' To this the answer is undoubtedly, 'Yes, but the results are harder to detect, since, if there were a total failure of technical ability, the inspiration would have faded, leaving no evidence of its existence.' You can find examples of clumsiness in expression by poets such as Clare and Hardy, but these seem only to enhance their real merits. You can find what appears to be whimsicality or archaism or affectation in the language of De la Mare and his contemporaries, and while you may regret them, you feel that they are part of the men and their work; accordingly you accept them as inevitable. After all, no poet is perfect, or we would wish all poets to be like him. On the contrary, we wish all poets to be as different from each other as possible. A poet aims, not at reaching some external and objective standard of perfection in his work, but at making it the best expression he can of his own poetic ideals. He may admit that Shakespeare was the greatest poet who ever lived, but he doesn't wish to write exactly like Shakespeare. He may aspire to make his poems as vital, moving and immediate as Shakespeare's were, but he knows he can do this only by expressing himself, not by imitating Shakespeare.

Let us take another example of technique in action. Alexander Pope, early in life, set himself the ideal of 'correctness'—that is, technical perfection. He set himself narrow limits, in the formal sense, by confining himself almost entirely to the heroic couplet, already perfected by the older master, Dryden. He attempted to achieve within this form as much variety as his nature demanded. He strove, in other words, to express the whole of himself through this medium. Here is a well-known example, to remind you of the form of the heroic couplet.

> True wit is nature to advantage dressed,
> What oft was thought but ne'er so well expressed.

The couplet consists of two rhymed iambic pentameters, each line neatly balanced within itself. The choice of words forces us to make pauses within the lines, thus ensuring variety and the right emphasis. In the first line there is an almost imperceptible pause after 'wit', or perhaps you prefer to make it after 'nature'. In the second line there is a marked pause after 'thought', which ensures that the couplet is clinched by the last five words. Here is a longer passage, the famous character of Addison, of whom Pope was envious. Pope had already expressed the sense of the lines in

H

a prose letter, and this he liked so well that he versified it with the utmost correctness and lucidity he could command. The rhythm is grave and measured, suggesting a judicial denunciation; the language is chosen with skill and deliberation, to ensure the maximum effect for every epithet of condemnation. It is a masterly passage.

> Peace to all such! but were there one whose fires
> True genius kindles and fair fame inspires,
> Blest with each talent and each art to please
> And born to write, converse and live with ease:
> Should such a man, too fond to rule alone,
> Bear, like the Turk, no brother near the throne,
> View him with scornful yet with jealous eyes,
> And hate for arts that caused himself to rise;
> Damn with faint praise, assent with civil leer,
> And without sneering teach the rest to sneer;
> Willing to wound and yet afraid to strike,
> Just hint a fault and hesitate dislike;
> Alike reserved to blame or to commend,
> A timorous foe and a suspicious friend,
> Dreading e'en fools, by flatterers besieged,
> And so obliging that he ne'er obliged;
> Like Cato give his little Senate laws
> And sit attentive to his own applause;
> While wits and Templars ev'ry sentence raise,
> And wonder with a foolish face of praise;
> Who but must laugh if such a man there be?
> Who would not weep if Atticus were he?

But Pope was not always as correct and telling as this. He was a marvellously accomplished technician in much of his verse, but critics do not always recognize how often he failed to come up to his own exacting standards.

It is not always easy to know how high to rate technique in poetry. Often it seems to be no more than the avoidance of clumsiness and the achievement of an appearance of naturalness. What is it that continues to give us pleasure in Lovelace's *Going to the Wars*, however often we read it?

> Tell me not, sweet, I am unkind
> That from the nunnery

Of thy chaste breast and quiet mind
    To war and arms I fly.

True, a new mistress now I chase,
    The first foe in the field;
And with a stronger faith embrace
    A sword, a horse, a shield.

Yet this inconstancy is such
    As you too shall adore:
I could not love thee, dear, so much,
    Loved I not honour more.

We recognize the sentiment as artificial; we may almost say that Lovelace was adopting a pose. But he was a Cavalier and, whether or not their cause was right, the Cavaliers, many of them, did go to war for the sake of honour. Their motives, like other people's, were mixed, but the abstract ideal of honour, of loyalty to the King, was a source of inspiration. No doubt Lovelace's poem is studied and artificial, yet there is something thrilling in the very pose he adopts. Had his technique been unequal to the thought he was expressing, there would be no magic in the poem. The technical achievement in Lovelace's poem lies in its capacity to make so studied and artificial a sentiment sound the most natural thing in the world. The rhythm is regular without being mechanical; the rhymes, with the possible exception of 'nunnery' and 'fly' (though it is not certain how these words were pronounced in Lovelace's time), are smooth and easy; above all, the word-order is much as in prose speech, with almost no inversion. Only in the first stanza is the word-order not that of prose. As for the triumphant and paradoxical final stanza, the rhythm and the position of the words give the impression of absolute spontaneity. For all we know, Lovelace may have worked on the lines for hours, but they sound as if they were struck off in a moment of pure inspiration. The economy of language and the wit of such a sequence of images as 'nunnery', 'mistress' and 'embrace' are another source of attraction. You may say, 'But he was only striking an attitude', to which I can only answer, 'Yes, but how well he strikes it, and after all, it was an attitude for which, at the time of the Civil War, men were prepared to die.'

After considering *Going to the Wars*, you may be tempted to say that technique is of primary importance, because without the technique there would be no poem. In this instance you could almost say that the technique *is* the poem. In a sense this is always true. It is one of the paradoxes of poetry that, while poetry *is* technique, technique is not poetry, nor in itself does it much matter. As we have seen it is in a sense only the avoidance of clumsiness and the appearance of naturalness. Moreover, where it obtrudes, it is bad—or at any rate, it detracts from the interest of the poem. 'Ars est celare artem'—'Art is the concealment of art'. That seems to apply exactly to *Going to the Wars*; and where a poet's technique shows, resulting in clumsiness, the poem is that much the poorer—not much, perhaps, but enough for us to regret that the poet did not take more pains. 'Art', or technique, in poetry is bad when it shows too much, just as it is bad when it is inadequate. It is worth studying in some detail, because, without an understanding of its various aspects, we cannot go far in the criticism of poetry. We may appreciate a poet's technique instinctively—we may like 'the way he writes' without knowing why. But our appreciation will be deeper and surer if we have some knowledge of the technical processes involved in poetic creation.

You may think I have been sitting on the fence. Do I think technique important or not? Do I regard it as the enemy of inspiration? The truth, I think, is something like this: the inner urge or impulse to write a poem arising from some psychological pressure or disturbance, is essential. It is the source of inspiration. This force, or drive, is, however, ineffectual if it is not accompanied by a heightening of the poet's technical power. Inspiration, indeed, may come to a poet in the form of a heightened command of language, a heightened sense of rhythm, an increased facility with rhyme or metre. If the mind of a poet is in the proper state to write a true poem, his technical resources will match themselves to his inspiration, almost without effort on his part. Yet this may not happen continuously or powerfully enough to ensure that his poem writes itself, as it were automatically. A rhyme may have to be consciously sought; a rhythm may need to be deliberately changed; an unwanted jingle of consonants may have to be eliminated. This work of revision is unavoidable. How does a poet acquire the technical skill he needs? Most of it, I think, he acquires instinctively through reading other poets. He reads with an ear for technical resources—rhyme, rhythm, alliteration, and so on. From all the available resources he selects what he prefers, what appeals to him most, what suits his own purposes best, and thus his personal technique is formed. According to his temperament he will handle it with extreme care and deliberation or compose with spontaneity, even carelessness. An over-patient temperament may produce correct but dead verse. An over-hasty temperament may produce poems with moments of brilliance, but spoilt by serious blemishes.

Technique, then, is important only as it serves inspiration; a poet is a man with something to say. If his command over the resources of poetry is adequate, he will say it well. If, on the other hand, he has nothing to say, the mere painstaking exploitation of technique will not make what he writes true poetry. The more a poet knows of the 'art' of language, the better equipped he will be to profit by the onset of inspiration. The better, also, will he be able to revise and correct his work. He cannot study the technique of his trade too long and devotedly. If he is a true poet, indeed, he will never cease from studying it in whatever he reads and whatever he writes. He is always learning. The resources used in writing one poem will not satisfy the demands made by writing another. The aim of all technique is to make poems seem as natural, as inevitable as possible. I conclude by returning to the image of a flower. What is more natural than a wild flower, and yet, when you examine it, more exquisitely designed. It is this balance between naturalness and design which a poet strives to achieve, or achieves without striving.

CHAPTER 14

RHYTHM

The most important of a poet's technical resources is rhythm. It is connected with the most primitive, the most deeply ingrained impulses in our nature. You have only to consider the singing games of children or the tribal dances of primitive peoples to realize this. Adults in sophisticated societies have rediscovered their primitive roots in the rhythms of jazz. School children skip to the rhythm of

> Queenie, Queenie Caroline,
> Dipped her hair in turpentine,
> Turpentine to make it shine,
> Queenie, Queenie Caroline

or bounce balls to

> Harry Brown went to town
> To buy a pair of breeches;
> Every time he tumbled down
> He bursted all his stitches.

And there are other rhymes which may once have been connected with singing games, but which are now spoken or chanted for their own sake.

> My mother said
> I never should
> Play with the gypsies in the wood.
> If I did
> She would say
> 'Naughty little girl to dis-o-bey'.

So traditional is the accepted rhythm of 'My mother said' that, if you don't happen to know it already, you will almost certainly say it wrong. It is impossible to convey its true rhythm accurately by ordinary printing methods. It is heavily accented, and there are long pauses after each of the short lines—

> *My* mother *said* (pause)
> *I* never *should* (pause)

and so on.

Of course not all rhythm is as strongly marked as this. Indeed, once the public became more sophisticated, and silent reading took the place of public declamation, the rhythmical element in poetry tended to become less pronounced. Take, for instance, these lines from Cowper's poem *The Task*, written towards the end of the eighteenth century.

> Come, Evening, once again, season of peace;
> Return, sweet Evening, and continue long!
> Methinks I see thee in the streaky west,
> With matron-step slow-moving, while the night
> Treads on thy sweeping train; one hand employed
> In letting fall the curtain of repose
> On bird and beast, the other charged for man
> With sweet oblivion of the cares of day.

You will realize that rhythm has here become simply a gentle undercurrent, making it possible almost to read the lines like prose. But of course prose, too, is rhythmical in its way, and I shall have something to say about that later. For the present we are concerned with the much more strongly marked rhythm of simple verse. It is time to attempt a general definition of rhythm.

Rhythm comes from a Greek word meaning 'flow'. 'Flow' means movement from one point to another. Water flows along river beds; blood flows in our veins; crowds flow along city streets. Traffic flows, or is supposed to flow, along arterial roads. If the flow is absolutely regular, it can hardly be called rhythmical. Gas forced along a pipe under constant pressure cannot be said to flow rhythmically. It is better, perhaps, to think of rhythm as pulse: pulse means alternating periods of effort and relaxation. We run rhythmically by a series of movements of which each alternate one has the result of lifting our bodies forward, and every other one restores the body to a position from which the next effort is to be made. Without such alternations of effort and rest it is almost impossible to conceive of bodily movement. The beating of our hearts and the course of our breathing offer the most basic examples. When such movements cease, we are dead. Rhythm is life, you might say. Rhythm, then, is the alternation between periods of effort or tension and periods of rest or relaxation. The rhythms of our bodies are paralleled by the larger and slower rhythms of nature—night and day, summer and winter, heat and cold, storm and calm. Notice that the first two of these—the days and the seasons—occur in constant alternation; their rhythm is regular. The others—temperature and atmospheric conditions— alternate in most, if not all parts of the world, with extreme irregularity, conforming only to a general pattern. Rhythm may be regular or irregular. The more regular it is, the easier it is to perceive. In poetry we associate extreme regularity of rhythm with the simpler, more primitive types of verse.

What is the purpose of rhythm, then? Why is it fundamental to poetry? Life is rhythmical, and rhythm is life. Of all man's cultural activities, the dance is the most marked in rhythm. Indeed the rhythmic movement of the body in religious or quasi-religious activities is the basis of the dance. In earliest times tribal dances for this or that cultural purpose were often, if not invariably accompanied by chants. Such combinations of song and dance are still common in less sophisticated communities all over the world.

If words were meant to accompany rhythmic dancing, they had to be rhythmic themselves. This is the origin of rhythm in poetry. Even now, when western poetry has been divorced from its origins in the dance for hundreds of years, its rhythmic character still recalls these origins. The connection between poetry and the dance is preserved in the word 'ballad', which comes from the Latin 'ballare'—to dance.

Even when, at the time when our traditional ballads were evolving poetry was losing its connection with the dance (so far as western Europe was concerned), it still retained its strongly rhythmic character. This was partly because it remained essentially a *sung* performance. Ballads were songs, and this required a more or less regular rhythmical structure, so that the melody might be repeated, more or less unchanged, as many times as the ballad had stanzas. But there is another reason why poetry is rhythmical. It is intended to be *memorable*. Why is it that all school children possess a repertoire (a very large one if we include all recorded examples) of chance rhymes and scraps of verse which are handed down from generation to generation without ever being written down?[1] The truth is that it is easier to remember

> Thirty days hath September,
> April, June, and November

than 'April, June, September and November each have thirty days'. The rhythm of the verse becomes built in with the very structure of our minds in childhood; just as it is easier to learn mathematical tables if we chant them in rhythmic form.

> Six one are six,
> Six twos are twelve,
> Six threes are eighteen,
> Six fours are twenty-four,
> Six fives are THIR-ty
> (Pause for breath and continue.)

Progressive educationists tell us that this is all wrong nowadays; but this is how I learned my tables, and I know what eight twelves or seven nines are as readily as I can say my name!

But why, you may wonder, was not rhythm in verse dropped as soon as verse became a written and not a spoken activity? If rhythm makes verse memorable, why retain it when verse is written down and need not be remembered? Well, of course, it has been said that the biggest blow to poetry was struck by the invention of printing, whereby the means were offered to every-one to get copies of poems for themselves, which they could read silently whenever they wished. But poets have persisted in retain-ing the attractions of rhythm long after poetry came to be written and printed. It must have some other purpose than to serve the memory.

Poetry was originally connected, as I have said, not only with the chant, but also with the dance. The dance is accompanied

---

[1] They have been collected and published as *The Lore and Language of School Children* by Iona and Peter Opie (Oxford 1959). But school children still learn their rhymes by oral communication.

by a heightened sense of excitement. The occasions for dancing are those of greater intensity, physical or emotional, than ordinary everyday life. Though poetry has long been divorced in the western world from both the song and the dance, we still regard it as being reserved for occasions of special significance. Because of this element of rhythm and the emotional excitement derived from it, let me stress this point. To take a very simple example, an example out of the traditional poetry we have long reserved for children:

> All the birds of the air fell a-sighing and a-sobbing
> When they heard of the death of poor Cock Robin.

Let us put it another way: 'When they heard that Cock Robin had been killed, all the other birds were overcome with grief'. What is the difference? This is an important question, because on the answer turns the whole matter of the value of poetry. If you think there is no essential difference, you will never be convinced that poetry is of any special worth. We can agree that the prose version is a plain statement of fact, and that the verse version has rhythm, rhyme (of a sort), and a certain picturesqueness of phrasing which has been kept out of the prose version. 'Fell a-sighing and a-sobbing', we can agree, is more effective than 'were overcome with grief'. It is more graphic and concrete. But the main difference lies in the rhythm. Whether or not we know the traditional tune to *Cock Robin*, whether or not we say it in our heads or out loud, these two chorus-lines sing themselves inside our heads and create a quite different effect from the prose statement: they are, as we agreed, more 'effective'. And in what does this effectiveness really consist?

In the prose statement we merely acknowledge a fact: we accept it with our intelligence, and that is all. Much the same happens when we take note of a street sign: 'No through road'. But in reading the verse version, we take part in an act of mourning; we assent emotionally to the sadness of the occasion. If there were a collection in aid of the robin's widow, we should probably subscribe to it because we are moved. Our emotions, not merely our intelligence, are involved. A poem, then, is an act, not simply a statement. This brings us back to what was said earlier—it is an

act of magic. And of the magic of the act rhythm is an essential
part. Listen for a minute to the rhythm of:

> This ae night, this ae night,
>   —Every night and all,
> Fire and fleet and candle-light,
>   And Christ receive thy soul.

> When thou from hence away art past,
>   —Every night and all,
> To Whinny-muir thou com'st at last,
>   And Christ receive thy soul.

> If ever thou gavest hosen and shoon,
>   —Every night and all,
> Sit thee down and put them on,
>   And Christ receive thy soul.

> If hosen and shoon thou ne'er gav'st nane,
>   —Every night and all,
> The whins shall prick thee to the bare bane,
>   And Christ receive thy soul.

> From Whinny-muir when thou may'st pass,
>   —Every night and all,
> To Brig o' Dread thou com'st at last;
>   And Christ receive thy soul.

> If ever thou gavest meat or drink,
>   —Every night and all,
> The fire shall never make thee shrink,
>   And Christ receive thy soul.

> If meat or drink thou ne'er gav'st nane,
>   —Every night and all,
> The fire will burn thee to the bare bane,
>   And Christ receive thy soul.

> This ae night, this ae night,
>   —Every night and all,
> Fire and fleet and candle-light,
>   And Christ receive thy soul.

This is the Cumberland Lyke-Wake chant—that is, a chant
used at the death-rites over a corpse, which was traditional in the

north of England as late as the seventeenth century. In the Middle
Ages it was customary for a dead man's relatives and their friends
to gather round the body and 'watch' through the night until the
burial next morning. The 'wake', as it was called, was often
accompanied by scenes of wild and sometimes orgiastic excitement, and it is easy to see how the emotional tension was raised
when a chant such as the one just quoted was sung, possibly by a
soloist and a chorus for the lines of the refrain. Apart from the
grim warning contained in the poem, the solemn liturgical rhythm
must have had a profound incantatory effect on the minds of the
hearers.

It may readily be understood that poets, once they had realized
the power of rhythm to enhance the magical effect of their lines,
should be unwilling to dispense with it. Indeed, it might be that,
once the song and dance element in poetry was discarded, the
necessity to retain rhythm would be even more pressing. Nevertheless, it must be admitted that, with the arrival of written
poetry, read silently, rhythm tended to become quieter, less
marked. This did not happen, however, until long after the invention of printing towards the end of the fifteenth century. For one
thing, the Tudor lyric was usually, if not invariably, composed to
be sung to the lute or the virginals, while much of the greatest
of Elizabethan verse, excluding lute songs, was written to be
declaimed on the stage. We shall consider this stage verse in a
later chapter. Look, however, at some lines by one of the greatest
Elizabethan non-dramatic poets, Edmund Spenser. This is a passage from *Prothalamion*.

> With that I saw two swans of goodly hue
> Come softly swimming down along the lee;
> Two fairer birds I yet did never see;
> The snow, which doth the top of Pindus strew,
> Did never whiter show;
> Nor Jove himself, when he a swan would be,
> For love of Leda, whiter did appear;
> Yet Leda was (they say) as white as he,
> Yet not so white as these, nor nothing near;
> So purely white they were,
> That even the gentle stream, the which them bare,

Seemed foul to them, and bade his billows spare
To wet their silken feathers, lest they might
Soil their fair plumes with water not so fair,
And mar their beauties bright,
That shone as heaven's light.
Against their bridal day, which was not long:
Sweet Thames run softly till I end my song.

Spenser has got away altogether from the strongly marked ballad rhythms of earlier times, and has developed a subtler, more meditative music of his own. His great aim was to achieve sweetness of sound, as distinct from the rougher, even harsher music of popular poetry.

His younger contemporary, John Donne, in conscious reaction against Spenserian sweetness, which he considered artificial, composed in a deliberately abrupt, more rugged style, believing that the reader needed to be jerked to attention, not lulled to sleep. He could write smoothly if he wished, but he preferred the harsher, grittier tone we associate with him.

For every hour that thou wilt spare me now,
    I will allow,
Usurious God of Love, twenty to thee,
When with my brown, my grey hairs equal be;
Till then, Love, let my body reign, and let
Me travel, sojourn, snatch, plot, have, forget,
Resume my last year's relict: think that yet
    We'd never met.

The varieties of rhythm in English poetry between the Middle Ages and the twentieth century have been almost infinite, and it would be possible to fill many pages by multiplying examples, old and new. By nothing so much as by his rhythm can an original poet be recognized. It is his handwriting. It is also his chief technical resource. But in calling it 'technical', we must not overlook the fact that it is largely instinctive. It is as much part of each poet's individuality as his voice. Each of us has roughly the same speech-making apparatus—lungs, vocal chords, tongue, teeth and palate. But every voice is different: each has its peculiar resonance, pitch and timbre. Yet one thing must be borne in mind. Just as nobody can properly be said to have a tone of voice apart from what he does with it, so there is really no such thing as rhythm, only rhythmical utterance—words in rhythm. This is important because writers sometimes speak of rhythm as if it were something *applied* as it were externally to a poetic thought. The words come to the poet in their proper rhythmic form: rhythm and word and thought are inseparable. If in composition the rhythm of a line seems to the poet to be wrong, he will alter the words; in so doing he modifies the thought. He composes not only with his intellect, like a man writing a scientific thesis, he writes also with his ear; and if ear and mind do not support each other, the poem will fail—or more strictly, he may give up writing this particular poem as a bad job. Each word must not only convey his meaning, it must sound right in conjunction with the rest of the poem.

If a word sounds wrong to the poet, it will not be on account of the sound alone: it will be wrong in every way. You cannot have in a poem a word which sounds wrong and is right from the intellectual point of view; or a word which sounds right and has the wrong meaning. It is common enough, to be sure, to find poems in which words are used too much on account of their sound qualities; the poem will be deficient in intellectual or emotional content, and will in due time pall.

Rhythm, then, is the movement, the flow, the pulse of poetry. It cannot be isolated, except for purposes of general discussion, from meaning, any more than we can think of the flow of a stream without thinking of the water. It contributes greatly to the emotional effect of poetry, offering sometimes a drug, sometimes a stimulant, under the influence of which we more readily accept the poet's meaning and respond to his magic. When for instance we read the opening of Coleridge's *Kubla Khan*, we know instinctively that the experience we are about to enjoy was of special significance for the poet, and that the lines are rich in magical suggestion.

> In Xanadu did Kubla Khan
> A stately pleasure-dome decree:
> Where Alph, the sacred river, ran
> Through caverns measureless to man
> Down to a sunless sea.

Who can say whether rhythm is here used as a narcotic or as a stimulant? Undoubtedly language as well as rhythm contributes to the effect, yet without the peculiar movement of the lines they would not be so mysterious and suggestive.

I have here discussed only regular rhythm. It remains to say something of irregular or free verse. If you listen to a passage of prose for some time, you will notice that it has a certain characteristic flow or rhythm, though you could not beat time or tap your foot to it. Try reading aloud these few lines of verse, followed immediately by a sentence or two of the prose of John Ruskin.

> The woods decay, the woods decay and fall,
> The vapours weep their burthen to the ground,
> Man comes and tills the field and lies beneath,
> And after many a summer dies the swan.
> Me only cruel immortality
> Consumes: I wither slowly in thine arms,
> Here at the quiet limit of the world,
> A white-haired shadow roaming like a dream
> The ever silent spaces of the East,
> Far-folded mists and gleaming halls of morn.
>
> (Tennyson: *Tithonus*)

There was a rocky valley between Buxton and Bakewell, once upon a time, divine as the vale of Tempe; you might have seen the gods there, morning and evening—Apollo and all the sweet Muses of the light, walking in fair procession on the lawns of it, and to and fro among the pinnacles of its crags. You cared neither for gods nor grass, but for cash. You enterprised a railway through the valley, you blasted its rock away, heaped thousands of tons of shale into its lovely stream. The valley is gone and the gods with it, and now every fool in Buxton can be at Bakewell in half an hour and every fool in Bakewell at Buxton; which you think is a lucrative process of exchange, you fools everywhere!

At first you will find yourself falling 'out of step', so to speak. You will try to apply the regular rhythm of the lines by Tennyson to the irregular prose rhythm of Ruskin. This isn't a book about prose, and I shall not discuss prose rhythm here. But the point I want to make is that there is often a magical element and a rhythmic magic in prose. Here, for instance, is a passage from the King James bible. You will see at once that it has all the qualities of the poetry we have been talking about, except regular rhythm.

And David lamented with this lamentation over Saul and over Jonathan his son: The beauty of Israel is slain upon thy high places: how are the mighty fallen! Tell it not in Gath, publish it not in the streets of Askelon; lest the daughters of the Philistines rejoice, lest the daughters of the uncircumcized triumph. Ye mountains of Gilboa, let there be no dew, neither let there be rain upon you, nor fields of offerings: for there the shield of the mighty is vilely cast away, the shield of Saul as though he had not been anointed with oil.

Does a poem, then, require regular rhythm? We have already discussed poems by the greatest exponent of free verse, Walt Whitman, and seen how he uses the rhythms of speech, adapted to constitute his very personal idiom. A later poet, D. H. Lawrence, wrote a fair amount of poetry in regular, or near-regular, forms, but he felt most at home with the free verse rhythms he contrived for himself.

At evening, sitting on this terrace,
When the sun from the west, beyond Pisa, beyond the mountains of
    Carrara
Departs, and the world is taken by surprise . . .

When the tired flower of Florence is in bloom beneath the glowing
Brown hills surrounding . . .

When under the arches of the Ponte Vecchio
A green light enters against stream, flush from the west,
Against the current of obscure Arno . . .

Look up, and you see things flying
Between the day and the night;
Swallows with spools of dark thread sewing the shadows together.

Nor is the dividing-line between regular verse and free verse so marked as we sometimes think owing to the different appearance of the two kinds of verse in print. A good deal of free verse is very similar to rhythmically regular verse, and a good deal of rhythmical verse has almost to be read as free verse. It is not always easy to draw a rigid dividing-line.

This is about as far as we can go with rhythm without introducing those other closely complementary terms, metre and language. Before doing so, it might be worth reading a passage by William Blake which is always printed as prose but could almost as easily have been presented as unrhymed verse.

Majestical she steppeth, and with her pure quill on every flower writeth Wisdom's name. Now lowly bending, whispers in mine ear, 'O man, how great, how little thou! O man, slave of each moment, lord of eternity! seest thou where Mirth sits on the painted cheek? doth it not seem ashamed of such a place, and grow immoderate to brave it out? O what an humble garb true Joy puts on! Those who want Happiness must stoop to find it; it is a flower that grows in every vale. Vain foolish man, that roams on lofty rocks, where, 'cause his garments are swoln with wind, he fancies he is grown into a giant! Lo then, Humility take it, and wear it in thine heart; lord of thyself, thou then art lord of all.'

CHAPTER 15

METRE

Metre, meaning 'measure', is the name given to the formal rhythmical patterns in which poetry is written. Rhythm, as I have explained, is a general term applying to all movement or flow in which a pulse is perceptible. Metre applies solely to verse. You could say that the beating of your heart is rhythmical, or that the throb of an engine is rhythmical, but not that they are metrical. Rhythm is the larger, more general term; metre, the smaller, more particular.

Metrical patterns vary in the writing of different languages. English metre is determined by stress. English, like German, is a heavily stressed language; French and Italian less so. English is so heavily stressed that the unstressed syllables almost disappear. For instance, the middle syllable of that word 'disappear' (represented by 'ap') is hardly pronounced at all, because 'dis-' and '-pear' take almost all the stress. Compare the pronunciation of 'inevitable circumstances' with that of the French 'les circonstances inévitables'. In the latter every syllable is given some weight; the stress is spread rather evenly over the whole phrase. But in the English two syllables only out of the nine are heavily stressed, '-ev-' and 'cir-', and the remaining seven are spoken lightly, almost indistinguishably. This is one reason why English people tend to speak badly, and anyone who takes the trouble to speak clearly is liable to be thought affected. An Englishman who has had dramatic training is usually somewhat conspicuous off the stage; most Frenchmen sound as if they might be actors.

This quality of being heavily stressed, though it makes English a difficult language for everyday speech, makes it an ideal language for metrical verse. It is capable of great rhythmic subtlety and variety. It lends itself equally well to the solemn pace of Gray's *Elegy* and the tripping lightness of Ariel's song in *The Tempest*, 'Where the bee sucks'.

However, in spite of the richness and variety of rhythm in English poetry, it is based on a surprisingly limited metrical foundation. To give it its technical name, this foundation is the *iamb*, or in Latin 'iambus'. This is a foot, or unit, consisting of one unstressed (weak) syllable, followed by one stressed (strong) syllable. A succession of iambs gives the familiar *ti-tum* rhythm which is the basis of most English verse. Quote what you like:

> To be or not to be, that is the question

or

> The proper study of mankind is man

or

> I wandered lonely as a cloud

or

> Where wealth accumulates and men decay

or

> And did those feet in ancient time

or

> A thing of beauty is a joy for ever

or

> The King sits in Dunfermline town;

and you will find this basic iambic pattern underlying the rhythm. Each line has its irregularities. If it had not, the result would be sheer monotony, and the reader would nod and eventually fall asleep. But the iamb—the *ti-tum* sound—is the basis of English versification. I have no statistics to hand, but I would guess that well over ninety per cent, perhaps ninety-nine, conforms to this pattern.

The unit of rhythm is called a 'foot'. Five iambic feet make up an iambic pentameter. A succession of iambic pentameters is called blank verse, and its popularity is due to its having been adopted as the normal form in the verse drama of the Elizabethan stage.

> Now walk the angels on the walls of Heaven,
> As sentinels to warn th' immortal souls
> To entertain divine Zenocrate:
> Apollo, Cynthia, and the ceaseless lamps
> That gently looked upon this loathsome earth,
> Shine downwards now no more, but deck the heavens
> To entertain divine Zenocrate.

Here you have some lines from Marlowe's *Tamburlaine*, where you may hear the iambic pentameter at its most regular and resonant. Once such a form had triumphantly established itself in the public ear, it is difficult to imagine its ever being replaced. We shall be dealing with blank verse in a later chapter.

The five-foot iambic line—the pentameter—did not, however, establish itself in England as early as another iambic form called ballad metre.

> There lived a wife at Usher's Well,
>   A wealthy wife was she;
> She had three stout and stalwart sons,
>   And sent them o'er the sea.
>
> They hadna been a week from her,
>   A week but barely ane,
> When word came to the carlin wife,
>   That her three sons were gane.
>
> They hadna been a week from her,
>   A week but barely three,
> When word came to the carlin wife,
>   That her sons she'd never see.

This is part of *The Wife of Usher's Well*, and if you sing-song it to yourself, you will see that each stanza consists of four lines, of which the first and third are four-foot iambic lines and the second and fourth are three-foot iambic lines. The first and third sometimes rhyme, and the second and fourth usually rhyme. This is a peculiarly satisfying metre to the English ear, and has never lost its popularity. It is the basis of folk verse, but its use has extended into sophisticated poetry at all times since the Middle Ages. You will remember the lines by the seventeenth century Cavalier poet, Richard Lovelace:

> Yet this inconstancy is such
>   As you too shall adore:
> I could not love thee, dear, so much,
>   Loved I not honour more.

This is in ballad metre, though the poem could not be called a ballad. When Wordsworth and Coleridge published their *Lyrical Ballads*, a hundred and fifty years after Lovelace, and three or four centuries after the traditional ballads, they used this same metre, among others; Wordsworth wrote:

> I met a little cottage girl,
> She was eight years old, she said;
> Her hair was thick with many a curl
> That clustered round her head.
>
> She had a rustic, woodland air,
> And she was wildly clad;
> Her eyes were fair, and very fair,
> —Her beauty made me glad.

And Coleridge composed the whole of his great *Rime of the Ancient Mariner* in ballad metre. He used it with consummate skill and a wonderful ear for subtle variations, but essentially it is the same metre as that of *Sir Patrick Spens*, *The Wife of Usher's Well* and *The Daemon Lover*:

> And now all in mine own Countree
>   I stood on the firm land!
> The Hermit stepped forth from the boat,
>   And scarcely he could stand.
>
> 'O shrive me, shrive me, holy Man!'
>   The Hermit crossed his brow—
> 'Say quick,' quoth he, 'I bid thee say
>   What manner of man art thou?'
>
> Forthwith this frame of mine was wrenched
>   With a woeful agony,
> Which forced me to begin my tale
>   And then it left me free.

It would take too long to enumerate the varieties of the ballad metre. Poets at all times have shown how they can take the essential form and adapt it to their peculiar needs. Keats, for instance, in the poem already quoted, *La Belle Dame Sans Merci*, adopted a form which he found in early Tudor poetry, and which had been adapted from the ballad metre. The first three lines of every stanza each have four iambic feet, and the fourth line has two feet only, as if to compensate for the extra length of the second line (which usually only has three feet).

> 'O what can ail thee, knight-at-arms,
>   Alone and palely loitering?
> The sedge has withered from the lake,
>   And no birds sing.'

This short final line has the effect of slowing up the reading at the end of each stanza and thus adding to the dramatic effect of the poem.

Another very popular form is what is usually called, somewhat clumsily, octosyllabic couplets. This consists of an indefinite number of lines, rhyming in pairs, each made up of four iambic feet. Here is part of Milton's *Il Penseroso*:

> There in close covert by some brook,
> Where no profaner eye may look,
> Hide me from day's garish eye,
> While the bee with honied thigh,
> That at her flowery work doth sing
> And the waters murmuring
> With such consort as they keep,
> Entice the dewy-feathered sleep;
> And let some strange mysterious dream,
> Wave at his wings in airy stream,
> Of lively portraiture displayed
> Softly on my eye-lids laid.

It might be thought that this pattern is suitable only for the lighter kinds of verse. But it has been used in poems of the most passionate and serious kind. Here, for instance, are a few lines from Andrew Marvell's *To his Coy Mistress*:

> Thy beauty shall no more be found,
> Nor in thy marble vault shall sound
> My echoing song; then worms shall try

That long-preserved virginity,
And your quaint honour turn to dust,
And into ashes all my lust:
The grave's a fine and private place,
But none, I think, do there embrace.

And here are four couplets from William Blake's great *Auguries of Innocence*:

He who mocks the infant's faith
Shall be mocked in age and death.
He who shall teach the child to doubt
The rotting grave shall ne'er get out.
He who respects the infant's faith
Triumphs over Hell and death.
The child's toys and the old man's reasons
Are the fruits of the two seasons.

Of the regular, traditional forms of English metre these three—the iambic pentameter, ballad metre, and the octosyllabic couplet—are much the most common. Lines having less than four or more than five feet are less common: shorter lines tend to be jerky, and longer tend to be monotonous. Some poets have written superbly in three-foot lines. For instance, here is part of a poem by Sir Walter Ralegh, attacking Tudor court society as he knew it. There is a kind of sardonic terseness about these brief and telling lines, but this is obviously a metre of limited use.

Tell zeal it wants devotion;
Tell love it is but lust:
Tell time it is but motion;
Tell flesh it is but dust:
And wish them not reply,
For thou must give the lie.

Tell age it daily wasteth;
Tell honour how it alters;
Tell beauty how she blasteth;
Tell favour how it falters:
And as they shall reply,
Give every one the lie.

John Skelton, a country priest and tutor to the young Henry

VIII, also excelled in the writing of poems in short lines. These have as a rule two or three stresses, but they are metrically very free, giving the impression of speed and spontaneity. Here are a few lines from his *Elinor Rumming*, a headlong account of a country ale-wife and her customers:

> But to make up my tale,
> She breweth nappy ale,
> And maketh thereof pot-sale
> To travellers, to tinkers,
> To sweaters, to swinkers,
> And all good ale-drinkers,
> That will nothing spare
> But drink till they stare
> And bring themselves bare,
> With 'Now away the mare!
> And let us slay care'

As for lines longer than the pentameter, consider the opening of Tennyson's *Locksley Hall*.

Comrades, leave me here a little, while as yet 'tis early morn:
Leave me here, and when you want me, sound upon the bugle-horn.
'Tis the place, and all around it, as of old, the curlews call,
Dreary gleams about the moorland flying over Locksley Hall.

Lines like these tend to break up into two, and might as well be printed thus:

> Comrades, leave me here a little
> While as yet 'tis early morn:
> Leave me here, and when you want me,
> Sound upon the bugle-horn.

Such a metre appealed to Tennyson, because he wanted to convey an effect of melancholy, and this he undoubtedly succeeded in doing. But perhaps you have already noticed that he has abandoned the customary iambic movement of English verse in favour of a different movement: ti-túm, in short, has become túm-ti. The accents fall on the first, not the second syllable, of each foot. We have moved away from the iamb and come to consider the *trochee*: that is, the metrical foot which consists of two syllables, the first strong and the second weak. The word 'trochee' is itself a trochee. A succession of trochees, as Longfellow discovered when writing *Hiawatha*, conveys an artificial, rather melancholy atmosphere; as his readers have discovered, it tends to unbearable monotony. Instead of quoting from Longfellow's all too well-known poem, here are some lines from Lewis Carroll's less familiar parody, *Hiawatha's Photographing*:

> All the while that she was sitting,
> Still the lady chattered, chattered,
> Like a monkey in the forest.
> 'Am I sitting still?' she asked him.
> 'Is my face enough in profile?
> Shall I hold the bouquet high?
> Will it come into the picture?'
> And the picture failed completely.

Both the basic feet we have so far considered, iambs and trochees, are of two syllables. It is worth noting that a trochee, of limited use as a basis for metre, is useful as an inversion of the iamb. Much iambic verse contains trochees as a means of securing variety, or allowing the poet liberty. Blake begins his poem *To the Muses* with a trochee, and the reader readily accepts this as part of a basically iambic movement.

> Whether on Ida's shady brow,
> Or in the chambers of the East,
> The chambers of the sun that now
> From ancient melody have ceased . . .

Shakespeare, in *Macbeth*, achieves many subtle variations on the basic iambic pentameter, and a line like 'Angels are bright still, though the brightest fell' is not felt to stray far from the iambic pattern.

All other metrical forms strike us as experimental, and only to be used in exceptional circumstances. Some poets, for instance, have wanted to achieve a galloping rhythm, and this is done by the use of *anapaests*. An anapaest is a three-syllable foot having two weak syllables followed by a strong one. Here is Byron describing the assault of the Assyrian cavalry on the tents of Sennacherib.

> The Assyrian came down like a wolf on the fold,
> And his cohorts were gleaming with purple and gold.

This anapaestic verse is felt to be artificial and rather crude in its effect. It is not easy to use without an appearance of flippancy, perhaps because it is the basis of the limerick.

> There was a young lady of Spain,
> Who was constantly sick in the train.

Indeed, when an anapaestic measure is used for a serious subject, it appears ill-chosen. When Cowper describes the fate of Alexander Selkirk, no one can feel that the metre is well chosen.

> I am monarch of all I survey;
> My right there is none to dispute.

Yes, anapaests are undoubtedly best reserved for frivolous subjects.

> The sexual urge of the camel
>   Is greater than anyone thinks,
> And can only be gratified fully
>   By going to bed with the Sphinx.
> Now the Sphinx has an external orifice
>   Which is choked by the sands of the Nile:
> Hence the hump on the back of the camel
>   And the Sphinx's inscrutable smile.

The complementary foot to the anapaest is the dactyl—one strong syllable followed by two weak ones. This is a classical foot and has met with little success in English. Only Shakespeare has achieved a memorable dactyllic line: 'Merrily, merrily, shall I live now.' Hood tried it in *The Bridge of Sighs*, but the result is something of a jingle.

> Make no deep scrutiny
> Into her mutiny
> Rash and undutiful:
> Past all dishonour
> Death has left on her
> Only the beautiful.

Enough has been said to show that the iambic foot is the *natural* unit of English verse. Attempts to make any other metrical unit the basis always have the air of experimentation, as if the poet were trying to be different for the sake of being different. Yet within the iambic range an astonishing variety of forms has been possible. We might list other metrical feet, such as the spondee (two strong syllables), but it would be more interesting to quote two or three stanza forms and indicate the metrical composition of each in turn. There is literally no limit to the possible combinations of metrical lines which can be made to form a stanza, and poets at various times have delighted in inventing or adapting stanza forms to their peculiar needs and fancies. For instance, this is the stanza form used by Herrick in *To Daffodils*:

> Fair daffodils, we weep to see
> You haste away so soon;
> As yet the early-rising sun
> Has not attained his noon.
> Stay, stay
> Until the hasting day
> Has run
> But to the evensong;
> And, having prayed together, we
> Will go with you along.

The stanza begins in ballad form (alternate four- and three-foot iambic lines); these are followed by a line consisting of a single spondee ('Stay, stay'), which has the effect of retarding the pace. Then comes a three-foot iambic line, then a single iamb ('Has run'), followed by another three-foot iambic line. The stanza ends with a return to the opening ballad pattern—a four-foot followed by a three-foot iambic line. In this way the stanza is rounded off, and the ear carried back to the beginning.

Here is a stanza from Shelley's *To a Skylark*:

> We look before and after,
> And pine for what is not:
> Our sincerest laughter
> With some pain is fraught;
> Our sweetest songs are those that tell of saddest thought.

Here we have four three-foot lines followed by a six-foot line; there is some ambiguity as to whether the basic movement is iambic or trochaic: in this particular stanza it is mainly iambic, though the fourth line has a tendency to the trochaic. In other stanzas the movement is more markedly trochaic—the stressed syllable precedes the unstressed:

> Higher still and higher
> From the earth thou springest.

This metrical freedom reflects the freedom enjoyed by the skylark.

Finally, here is the first stanza of Hardy's *Weathers*:

> This is the weather the cuckoo likes,
>   And so do I;
> When showers betumble the chestnut spikes,
>   And nestlings fly:
> And the little brown nightingale bills his best,
> And they sit outside at *The Traveller's Rest*.
> And maids come forth sprig-muslin drest,
> And citizens dream of the south and west,
>   And so do I.

This is an excellent example of Hardy's originality as an inventor of lyric forms. He begins with a four-foot followed by a two-foot line, and repeats this pattern. He then has four four-foot lines, concluding with a two-foot line. The two-foot lines are in each case iambic, but the four-foot lines vary between an iambic and an anapaestic movement. This variety conveys the informal, speech-like quality of Hardy's tone.

As a tireless innovator in stanza forms, Hardy took as much delight in evolving fresh patterns as any seventeenth-century lyrist. Yet we rarely, if ever, feel that he innovates for the sake of novelty: it is almost always in response to some inner need of what he is trying to convey. Who does not feel, for instance, how entirely appropriate to the mood of *A Broken Appointment* is the stanza form evolved for that poem, where the slow two-foot opening line, echoed at the end of the stanza, is like a tolling bell sounding the doom of the poet's hopes?

> You did not come,
> And marching Time drew on, and wore me numb.—
> Yet less for loss of your dear presence there
> Than that I thus found lacking in your make
> The high compassion which can overbear
> Reluctance for pure lovingkindness' sake
> Grieved I, when, as the hope-hour stroked its sum,
>   You did not come.

What is the present situation of metre in poetry? Like so many other things, this element of poetic creation is in the melting-pot. Anything goes. The effect of free verse has been, even where a poet writes more or less regularly, to loosen the traditional forms and makes them less formal, less regular. A contemporary poet feels himself free to adopt an old form, contrive a new one, or employ a combination of new and traditional patterns. We live, as has been said, in a literary museum, where all the resources of the past are available, and there is no compulsion from fashion or usage to adopt or ignore any of them. The test of every poem is therefore in itself, not in the degree of its conformity to accepted rules. The present, then, is a time in which it is easier for a mediocre poet to write a passable poem and harder for a true poet to write a good one.

CHAPTER 16

BLANK VERSE

Success in poetic technique depends on a balance between freedom and restraint. One of the difficulties felt by modern poets is that there are now no accepted restrictions. A poet has complete freedom to write rhymed or unrhymed verse, to use regular stanza-forms or none, to invent his own new and personal rhythms or borrow the tighter rhythms of other poets. He may use the sonnet-form if he wants to, but there is no special virtue in so doing; if he uses it, he can modify it in a way which no poet in Milton's time would have dreamed of. But at some former times poets have felt the weight of excessive restriction. In the eighteenth century Pope and his followers had imposed a conception of 'correctness' on English verse which the Romantic poets of a later generation had to throw off. The Victorians accepted, if they did not impose, certain conventions which the poets of our century had to discard. In general, an age where new ideas are appearing is likely to be one in which new poetic forms will also appear. One such age was what we call the Renaissance.

The Renaissance, which involved a breakaway from medieval ideas and brought a new sense of power, opportunity and expansion to artists and progressively-minded people in all the western nations, came to England in the time of the Tudor monarchs. English poetry, which had made little progress in the century after the death of Chaucer, was slow to reach its full flowering. It was not until the last quarter of the sixteenth century—the latter part of Queen Elizabeth's reign—that it attained that strength and richness we associate with the word 'Elizabethan'. Something has been said about the lyric—that bursting-out of the sheer desire to sing in words—and also of the sonnet. But the most characteristic expression of the Elizabethan poetic genius was in the drama.

It has already been said that the somewhat elaborate rhyme-scheme of the sonnet, as we derived it from Italy, was found by many poets to have a too restricting influence. Many marvellous sonnets were written during this quarter-century, and the general level is high. But when poets wrote for the stage, they felt that rhyme was, for the most part, a hampering device. On the stage they wished to represent men and women in action, speaking, it is true, not exactly as they spoke in real life, but in a style sufficiently free and natural to allow full scope to the expression of feeling. Moreover, stage speech had to be fairly swift; it was not to be lingered over as a singer to the lute might linger over a brief lyric. Shakespeare was not the first Elizabethan to write fine plays for the stage; but it was during his career—roughly speaking, the thirty years following 1580—that Elizabethan stage verse achieved complete maturity.

'But why', you might say, 'write plays in verse? Why not prose? This is how people actually speak.' To answer briefly and simply: except for some comedies, Elizabethan plays were not about the man in the street; they were about great persons—kings and queens, statesmen, nobles and generals. It was the convention that such people spoke in a more elevated way than ordinary people. How else was the feeling to be conveyed that their actions and thoughts were important? Most of the subjects of tragedy and history, and even many of those of comedy, were given the dignity of verse. Shakespeare did indeed use prose, but mainly as a contrast to verse, in certain well-defined situations. He wrote excellent stage prose, having the ring of real, down-to-earth speech, but it was reserved for low or comic characters—Dogberry, the gravediggers or Falstaff—or for other characters under stress of severe psychological tension, as at times of mental derangement. Ophelia talks prose in her madness, so does Lady Macbeth when she walks in her sleep. It would be tempting to say that Shakespeare used prose when he required a lowering of emotional tension; but on some occasions it seems actually to heighten the tension.

The line the Elizabethans took as their norm was the iambic pentameter. At first, a good deal of rhyme was used, as in Shakespeare's earlier plays: here are a few lines from *A Midsummer Night's Dream*:

And in the wood, where often you and I
Upon faint primrose-beds were wont to lie,
Emptying our bosoms of their counsel sweet,
There my Lysander and myself shall meet;
And thence from Athens turn away our eyes,
To seek new friends and stranger companies.
Farewell, sweet playfellow: pray thou for us;
And good luck grant thee thy Demetrius!—
Keep word, Lysander: we must starve our sight
From lovers' food till morrow deep midnight.

As you can see—or rather, hear—this is somewhat artificial
and seems to slow up the action and linger unduly on the poetry.
Accordingly Shakespeare, in common with other dramatists—
Marlowe, Chapman and the rest—soon discarded rhyme and
made the unrhymed iambic pentameter his normal unit. This is
what we call *blank verse*.

Like most features of English poetry, blank verse had somewhat obscure and inauspicious historical beginnings. The origin
of blank verse in English is usually attributed to the Earl of
Surrey who, it is not clear why, adopted it—or hit on it—for use in
a translation of Virgil's *Aeneid*. Here is the beginning of Book II:

They whisted all, with fixèd face attent,
When prince Aeneas from the royal seat
Thus gan to speak. O Queen! it is thy will
I should renew a woe cannot be told:
How that the Greeks did spoil, and overthrow
The Phrygian wealth and wailful realm of Troy:
Those ruthful things that I myself beheld;
And whereof no small part fell to my share.
Which to express, who could refrain from tears?
What Myrmidon? or yet what Dolopes?
What stern Ulysses' wagèd soldier?
And lo! moist night now from the welkin falls;
And stars declining counsel us to rest.
But since so great is thy delight to hear
Of our mishaps, and Troyè's last decay;
Though to record the same my mind abhors,
And plaint eschews, yet thus will I begin.

Still, the sources of great rivers are often obscure and unexciting. The stream did not grow much bigger or deeper for many years after Surrey's time. But with Marlowe it became a mighty flood.

> Nature that framed us of four elements,
> Warring within our breasts for regiment,
> Doth teach us all to have aspiring minds:
> Our souls, whose faculties can comprehend—
> The wondrous Architecture of the world:
> And measure every wand'ring planet's course,
> Still climbing after knowledge infinite,
> And always moving as the restless Spheres,
> Will us to wear ourselves and never rest,
> Until we reach the ripest fruit of all,
> That perfect bliss and sole felicity,
> The sweet fruition of an earthly crown.

Such a movement, it must be admitted, is intoxicating. Was not this the ideal medium in which to stride about the stage declaiming noble thoughts, wrangling with an enemy, or even making love—when this had to be done in public? Marlowe's blank verse, it must be owned, was often a little stiff. It was splendid for his purpose, but it lacked the flexibility required for full variety of mood and character. It was Shakespeare's task to make it the perfect instrument for his unequalled dramatic achievement—the revelation of every kind of character in every possible psychological situation. He can make it move swiftly or ponderously: he can suggest a whisper or a roar; he can recount an incident, represent a display of crossfire wit; reveal ambition, lust, suspicion, remorse, self-accusation, rapture, scorn and anger. He did, indeed, strain the limits of the regular blank verse form, as if his thoughts refused to be contained within arbitrary bounds, especially in his later plays. Shakespeare was an actor, and he had had his training on the boards. Accordingly he had developed the most sensitive ear for language of which we have any knowledge. He used the blank verse lines with a natural mastery that can only be called miraculous. We have no space to illustrate the almost endless variety of Shakespeare's blank verse. As brief samples, here are three passages—one from an early play, one from the middle period and one from a late play. Brief as these

K

are, they will be enough to give an idea of the amazing development of Shakespeare's verse in the direction of flexibility and natural eloquence. Here is part of a speech from the beginning of *Romeo and Juliet*:

> Three civil brawls, bred of an airy word,
> By thee, old Capulet, and Montague,
> Have thrice disturbed the quiet of our streets;
> And made Verona's ancient citizens
> Cast-by their grave beseeming ornaments,
> To wield old partisans, in hands as old,
> Cankered with peace, to part your cankered hate:
> If ever you disturb our streets again,
> Your lives shall pay the forfeit of the peace.
> For this time, all the rest depart away:—
> You, Capulet, shall go along with me;—
> And, Montague, come you this afternoon,
> To know our further pleasure in this case,
> To old Freetown, our common judgement-place.—
> Once more, on pain of death, all men depart.

Here are some lines from *Troilus and Cressida*:

> What, am I poor of late?
> 'Tis certain, greatness, once faln out with fortune,
> Must fall out with men too: what the declined is,
> He shall as soon read in the eyes of others
> As feel in his own fall; for men, like butterflies,
> Show not their mealy wings but to the summer;
> And not a man, for being simply man,
> Hath any honour, but honour for those honours
> That are without him, as place, riches, favour,
> Prizes of accident as oft of merit:
> Which when they fall, as being slippery standers,
> The love that leaned on them as slippery too,
> Do one pluck down another, and together
> Die in the fall.

And finally, a passage from *The Winter's Tale*:

> Thou dearest Perdita,
> With these forced thoughts, I prithee, darken not
> The mirth o' the feast: or I'll be thine, my fair,

Or not my father's; for I cannot be
Mine own, nor any thing to any, if
I be not thine: to this I am most constant,
Though destiny say no. Be merry, gentle;
Strangle such thoughts as these with any thing
That you behold the while. Your guests are coming:
Lift up your countenance, as it were the day
Of celebration of that nuptial which
We two have sworn shall come.

To write blank verse requires but little skill. Its smooth iambic movement is not hard to imitate. A child can count five feet; there are no tiresome rhymes to tax your skill. You can churn out blank verse eternally, with very little effort—just like this.

That paragraph is, in fact, blank verse disguised as prose. I wrote it for you, with very little hesitation, just to show how simple it is. But it is bad blank verse, utterly without purpose or inspiration, and worse than even decent prose. Great blank verse drama died with the successors to the Elizabethans, and attempts to revive it for the Victorian stage were fruitless. The inspiration had gone out of it; the Elizabethan spell had long ago been broken. Tennyson and Browning, who both tried their hands at blank verse tragedy, as did other lesser men, had no first-hand knowledge of the stage; their dramatic verse, though in places vigorous enough, was still-born. We must look elsewhere than the theatre for blank verse after the time of Elizabeth and James I.

I have shown how simple it is to compose blank verse of sorts. If it is not inspired by some inner emotional pressure, or some sense of the dramatic, it will never get off the ground. Good blank verse, since its external rules are so few, and its external form so lacking in variety, requires a sensitive poetic instinct: in other words, an unusually good ear. This Milton undoubtedly had. In composing *Paradise Lost* he poured scorn upon rhyme as 'the invention of a barbarous age, to set off wretched matter and lame metre'. He adapted blank verse for his own purpose—that of reasoned argument and declamation. He departed altogether from the earlier Elizabethan manner and composed in paragraphs of several—sometimes many—lines. The following is from *Paradise Lost*, Book II:

'My sentence is for open war. Of wiles,
More unexpert, I boast not: them let those
Contrive who need, or when they need; not now.
For, while they sit contriving, shall the rest—
Millions that stand in arms, and longing wait
The signal to ascend—sit lingering here,
Heaven's fugitives, and for their dwelling-place
Accept this dark opprobrious den of shame,
The prison of his tyranny who reigns
By our delay? No! let us rather choose,
Armed with Hell-flames and fury, all at once
O'er Heaven's high towers to force resistless way,
Turning our tortures into horrid arms
Against the torturer; when, to meet the noise
Of his almighty engine, he shall hear
Infernal thunder, and, for lightning, see
Black fire and horror shot with equal rage
Among his angels, and his throne itself
Mixed with tartarean sulphur and strange fire,
His own invented torments . . .'

It is noteworthy how blank verse reflects a poet's nature. Milton's verse, like his character, was somewhat stiff, formal and severe. Yet Milton managed to achieve more variety than this perhaps implies. Yet even when he unbent, he did so with a certain self-consciousness. He never wrote relaxed or natural verse, as if he always found it difficult to be at ease.

After Milton's time blank verse underwent something of an eclipse in favour of rhymed iambic pentameters—heroic couplets—about which something will be said later. But it was revived towards the middle of the eighteenth century, and remained in favour until about the time of the 1914–18 war.

The function of blank verse, once it had left the theatre, was as a medium for long poems, and long poems remained in fashion throughout the period I have mentioned. It can of course become tedious, just as the ballad stanza became tedious in unskilled hands. It was used with success by many eighteenth-century poets—notably Akenside and Thomson—and again at the very end of the century by Wordsworth and Coleridge. Here is a passage from Wordsworth's account of his boyhood in *The Prelude*, Book I:

> And in the frosty season, when the sun
> Was set, and visible for many a mile
> The cottage windows blazed through twilight gloom,
> I heeded not their summons: happy time
> It was indeed for all of us—for me
> It was a time of rapture! Clear and loud
> The village clock tolled six,—I wheeled about,
> Proud and exulting like an untired horse
> That cares not for his home. All shod with steel,
> We hissed along the polished ice in games
> Confederate, imitative of the chase
> And woodland pleasures,—the resounding horn,
> The pack loud chiming, and the hunted hare.

And here is the opening to Coleridge's *Frost at Midnight*, written at about the same period:

> The frost performs its secret ministry,
> Unhelped by any wind. The owlet's cry
> Came loud—and hark, again! loud as before.
> The inmates of my cottage, all at rest,
> Have left me to that solitude, which suits
> Abstruser musings: save that at my side
> My cradled infant slumbers peacefully.
> 'Tis calm indeed! so calm, that it disturbs
> And vexes meditation with its strange
> And extreme silentness. Sea, hill and wood,
> This populous village! Sea, and hill, and wood,
> With all the numberless goings on of life,
> Inaudible as dreams! the thin blue flame
> Lies on my low burnt fire, and quivers not;
> Only that film, which fluttered on the grate,
> Still flutters there, the sole unquiet thing.

In these passages both poets speak with an intimate, personal voice far removed from declamation and theatrical effect.

In the nineteenth century blank verse was used extensively by almost every major poet. Tennyson had perhaps the best ear, and wrote much of his finest work in this form. Browning gave it a very characteristic note, much unlike other practitioners of blank verse. Perhaps in conscious reaction against Tennysonian smoothness, he deliberately broke up the lines and roughened the movement.

> And as yon tapers dwindle, and strange thoughts
> Grow, with a certain humming in my ears,
> About the life before I lived this life,
> And this life too, popes, cardinals and priests,
> Saint Praxed at his sermon on the mount,
> Your tall pale mother with her talking eyes
> And new-found agate urns as fresh as day,
> And marble's language, Latin pure, discreet,
> —Aha, ELUCESCEBAT quoth our friend?
> No Tully, said I. Ulpian at the best!
> Evil and brief hath been my pilgrimage.
> All *lapis*, all, sons! Else I give the Pope
> My villas! Will ye ever eat my heart?
>
> (*The Bishop Orders his Tomb at St Praxed's Church*)

Gradually, however, blank verse lost ground. For this there were two reasons. First, the resources of the form were becoming exhausted. After the middle of the century it was scarcely possible to write blank verse which did not sound like the work of a former poet. Secondly, by the end of the century the long poem was falling out of favour. The novel, which was the most characteristic literary form, pretty well took over narrative; no one wanted any more *Enoch Ardens* when they had the prose of Hardy, Meredith and George Eliot. Nor were long philosophical and reflective pieces in blank verse, such as Browning had produced, much more in demand. The public was becoming weary of sheer length. They preferred essays to be in prose. The decline of blank verse took many years. There were still poets in the twentieth century who turned out long blank verse narratives, but these found no lasting favour. It is after all possible for a literary form to exhaust itself after many years' use.

Surprisingly, perhaps, blank verse has died hardest in the United States. This is because of the example of the late Robert Frost, the last to achieve originality in this well-tried form. Whatever he wrote, his voice was his own; he employed considerable freedom, combined, however, with a strong underlying sense of the nature of the medium. Here is the conclusion to his famous *Death of the Hired Man*:

> 'But, Warren, please remember how it is:
> He's come to help you ditch the meadow.
> He has a plan. You mustn't laugh at him.
> He may not speak of it, and then he may.
> I'll sit and see if that small sailing cloud
> Will hit or miss the moon.'

> It hit the moon.
> Then there were three there, making a dim row,
> The moon, the little silver cloud, and she.

> Warren returned—too soon, it seemed to her,
> Slipped to her side, caught up her hand and waited.

> 'Warren?' she questioned.
> 'Dead,' was all he answered.

This almost takes blank verse back to the stage, where it had almost begun. Whether it will be revived on any large scale depends, like so many other things in poetry, on the personal practice of individual poets. Unpredictability is the essence of poetry. What is predictable is, in a sense, dead; and wherever there is life, there can be poetry. No one would dare to prophesy that some unborn poet will not re-discover the blank verse that began in the sixteenth century and adapt it to his own unique purposes.

CHAPTER 17

ALLITERATION, RHYME, ASSONANCE

What a poem says is of primary importance. A poem makes a statement or a declaration; it expresses a feeling or a mood; it relates a story or conveys an idea. These constitute meaning in poetry. But a poem is more than a statement, a declaration, a feeling, a mood, a story or an idea. If that were all, prose would be enough. A poem *is* itself; it is an act of magic, an imaginative creation. No one can analyse its magic fully. One thing we can say, however: a poem is made up of words. Words have not only meaning, but also form and sound. Any account of poetry which does not discover in it an element of *playing with words* is inadequate. Sometimes this play element is large, as in nursery rhymes; sometimes it is small. But if it is not there, we are reading prose. If the play element is so large as almost or wholly to exclude meaning, we have nonsense. The English language contains some excellent nonsense poetry.

> 'Twas brillig, and the slithy toves
>   Did gyre and gimble in the wabe;
> All mimsy were the borogoves,
>   And the mome raths outgrabe.
>
> 'Beware the Jabberwock, my son!
>   The jaws that bite, the claws that catch!
> Beware the Jubjub bird, and shun
>   The frumious Bandersnatch!'
>
> He took his vorpal sword in hand:
>   Long time the manxome foe he sought—
> So rested he by the Tumtum tree,
>   And stood awhile in thought.
>
> And as in uffish thought he stood,
>   The Jabberwock, with eyes of flame,
> Came whiffling through the tulgey wood,
>   And burbled as it came!

One, two! One, two! And through and through
    The vorpal blade went snicker-snack!
He left it dead, and with its head
    He went galumphing back.

'And hast thou slain the Jabberwock?
    Come to my arms, my beamish boy!
O frabjous day! Callooh! Callay!'
    He chortled in his joy.

'Twas brillig, and the slithy toves
    Did gyre and gimble in the wabe;
All mimsy were the borogoves,
    And the mome raths outgrabe.

Everyone knows the nonsense poems of Lewis Carroll and Edward Lear. Many will feel, as I do, that 'nonsense' is not altogether the right word. You cannot say that in *Jabberwocky*, just quoted, there is not a considerable suggestion of meaning. Carroll wants to recount an imaginary combat between a boy and a monster, half-legend, half-nightmare, and to convey the sense of terror and suspense it evokes. He accordingly disconnects the narrative from everyday affairs by the initial stanza, clearly less meaningful, more nonsensical than the stanzas which follow. He concludes the poem with a return to the same statement, so full of ominous suggestion.

As a matter of fact, he does explain "Twas brillig and the slithy toves' elsewhere. He tells us that 'brillig' means 'Four o'clock in the afternoon (the time when you're broiling things for dinner)' and that 'slithy' means 'lithe and slimy'; 'tove' is 'a creature resembling a badger, a lizard, and a corkscrew, that nests under sun-dials and lives on cheese'; 'gyre' means 'go round and round like a gyroscope'; 'gimble' is to 'make holes like a gimlet'; 'wabe' is 'a grass plot round a sun-dial'. 'Mimsy' means 'flimsy and miserable'; a 'borogove' is 'a thin shabby-looking bird with its feathers sticking out all round—something like a live mop'. 'Mome raths'—'a sort of green pig, but *mome* I am not certain about. I think it's short for "from home"—meaning that they'd lost their way, you know.' 'Outgrabe'—'made a noise something between bellowing and whistling, with a kind of sneeze in the middle'.

This is good fun, but it hardly destroys the impression that we are listening to a sort of meaningful nonsense, a spell in a foreign tongue. Carroll was playing with words, as you may hear a child play with sounds when he has scarcely learnt to speak. Good poetry always has an element—even though often only a trace—of 'jabberwocky', as we may call it—meaningful and spell-binding nonsense. Look again at the opening of *Kubla Khan*, and you will see what I mean.

> In Xanadu did Kubla Khan
> A stately pleasure-dome decree:
> Where Alph, the sacred river, ran
> Through caverns measureless to man
> Down to a sunless sea.

This clearly announces a magical experience of profound significance, and by its sheer sound qualities it produces in the reader that 'willing suspension of disbelief' which Coleridge described as the prerequisite to the enjoyment of poetry. Look more closely at these five lines of Coleridge, You will see that part of the sound quality of the lines comes from the rhyme-scheme: lines 1, 3 and 4 rhyme with each other; line 2 rhymes with line 5. It is not necessary to define rhyme; everyone can recognize it. In traditional poetry, composed to be sung or spoken, rhyme was not always exact; written poetry demands a close approximation to exactness. In the five lines we are examining exact rhyme only occurs if we pronounce 'Khan' to rhyme with 'man'. I think Coleridge meant it to be so pronounced: it seems to me more satisfying that way. The reason for this is that, not only is there a rhyme at the end of the line, there is also an internal rhyme: in fact, a pair of internal rhymes, which create an almost musical effect. 'Xan-' rhymes with 'Khan', and '-du' with 'Ku-'. Say the line aloud and you will instantly hear what I mean. This first line seems, then, to do two things: it directs your mind to the legendary oriental conqueror who was noted for his power and the splendour of his creations; it suggests also that the experience you are to share in is one of profound magical significance. I am not concerned here with the question how far this was Coleridge's conscious purpose; I hardly think that matters. I am inclined to think that his purpose was unconscious; otherwise it might not have been so successful: we are all too familiar with the too deliberate efforts of some poets to create a magical atmosphere. I am not forgetting that Coleridge tells us he wrote this poem in a trance brought about by taking opium. In this case the effects would have been achieved unconsciously. However, I am not convinced that the story he tells of the composition of *Kubla Khan* was not slightly exaggerated. He did not relate it until a good many years after the poem was written.

Other sound-effects can hardly be missed, even on a silent reading of the lines. In each of the five lines there is a pair of words beginning with the same sound: 'Kubla' and 'Khan'; 'dome' and 'decree'; 'river' and 'ran'; 'measureless' and 'man'; 'sunless' and 'sea'. Was this accidental? I can hardly think so. But if it is deliberate, it is very artfully and subtly done, so as not to obtrude itself. Do you not feel, as I do, that when Tennyson composes word-music, as he so often does, his art does not sufficiently conceal itself, and we are aware of its artificiality?

> Sweeter thy voice, but every sound is sweet;
> Myriads of rivulets hurrying thro' the dawn,
> The moan of doves in immemorial elms,
> And murmuring of innumerable bees.

If a writer produces these effects consciously, with deliberate artifice, we are entitled to call him a good craftsman, a skilful versifier; only if he has much more to offer us can we call him a true poet. A true poet is likely to produce his effects without the air of self-consciousness. Keats said that 'If poetry comes not as naturally as leaves to a tree, it had better not come at all'. At the same time, unless there is a long tradition behind a poet, there is likely to be a need for conscious effort, even for a degree of artificiality. This at any rate is the impression we get from what is called *alliterative verse*.

I mentioned just now the alliteration in the opening lines of *Kubla Khan*. This might be described as a kind of beginning-rhyme, just as rhyme itself is end-rhyme. When we speak of two words rhyming, we mean they end with the same sound: 'ran' and 'man', 'holy' and 'lowly', 'tenderly' and 'slenderly'. But this conception of rhyme did not come into the poetry of England until comparatively late in our history. Chaucer, writing in the second half of the fourteenth century, was the first poet of national importance to use rhyme on a considerable scale. The poetry of those who wrote before him, and even of some who were contemporary with him, did not employ end-rhyme. In the unrhymed poetry written before Chaucer's time, poets were interested mainly in alliteration: beginning-rhyme, not end-rhyme. Medieval poets inherited this alliterative verse, as we now call it, from their Saxon ancestors. Alliterative verse also had its own peculiar rhythm, very unlike the rhythm which Chaucer adapted from Italian and French models. Alliterative rhythm was based, not on the iamb, but on the dactyl—a foot consisting of one stressed syllable followed by two unstressed. The effect in our ears is a little sing-song, a little monotonous; but the monotony is not unpleasing, especially when set off, as it is, by alliteration. Try the sound of a few lines (slightly modernized) from *The Vision of Piers Plowman* by Chaucer's contemporary, William Langland. It tells how Gluttony returns home after a spree at the local tavern:

> They sat so till evensong and sang for a while,
> Till Glutton had guzzled a gallon and a gill.
> He might neither step nor stand till he his staff had;
> Then began he to go, like a gleeman's bitch,
> Sometimes sideways and sometimes backwards,
> As one who lays lines to catch little birds.
> When he drew near the doorway his eyes grew dim;
> He stumbled on the threshold and sank to the floor.
> Clement the Cobbler caught him by the middle
> For to lift him aloft and laid him on his knees.
> With all the woe in the world his wife and his wench
> Bore him home to his bed and brought him therein,
> And after his excess he had a fit of sloth;
> He slept Saturday and Sunday till the sun went to rest.
> Then woke he from his winking and wiped his eyes,
> And the first word he uttered was, 'Where is my breakfast?'

This, you will agree, is vigorous in movement and striking in sound, though strange to modern ears. During the century which followed Chaucer's death, alliterative verse fell into disuse. It had had its day. But the instinct, as we may call it, for alliteration has always persisted in the English ear. It is built into our speech-habits. Proverbial expressions such as 'time and tide', 'hearth and home', 'storm and stress' bear witness to it. Inventors of advertising slogans are well aware of the potency of alliterative effects. Thus alliteration, like rhyme, persists in English poetry, even after its initial purpose has been superseded. For we cannot doubt that alliteration, like rhyme, was used as an aid to memory in the days before poetry was written down. But they have never been merely that. They are an essential, though often unobtrusive, element in the sound-pattern of poetry. Consider how both play their part in this song from Shakespeare's *Measure for Measure*.

> Take, O take those lips away,
>   That so sweetly were forsworn;
> And those eyes, the break of day,
>   Lights that do mislead the morn!
> But my kisses bring again,
>   Bring again;
> Seals of love, but sealed in vain,
>   Sealed in vain!

This is not quite so tightly organized as the lines from *Kubla Khan*, but the play of rhyme and alliteration is as subtle. It was this aspect of the song which led Housman to say of it, 'That is nonsense, but it is ravishing poetry'. I don't myself think that nonsense can be ravishing poetry; nor do I think this is nonsense. On the other hand, I wouldn't like to have to say precisely what the song means. I think there must be something in it which was understood by an Elizabethan audience, but cannot be understood by us. The difficulty is to reconcile the taking away of lips with the bringing back of kisses. It is a teasing problem, and one not to be solved, I feel sure, by regarding the lines as jabberwocky.

There are people who refuse to accept anything as a poem unless it rhymes. How often does a teacher still hear the words spoken of a piece of free verse, 'But it isn't poetry—it doesn't rhyme'. We have seen how this view is untenable. We know, from the example of numerous poets—Milton, Whitman, D. H. Lawrence, T. S. Eliot, not to mention the great dramatists and other writers of blank verse—that rhyme can be dispensed with.

Granted, however, that rhyme is not, and never has been, an essential constituent of English poetry, we have to admit the extraordinary fascination it exercises over our poets, and its strong and vigorous persistence in the poetry of today, when poets are impatient of mechanical devices and external disciplines. A check of the ten poems in three literary reviews which appeared last week reveals that six are rhymed, four unrhymed. One of those I have listed as 'rhymed' employs throughout a device known as *assonance*. This means half-rhyme or near-rhyme. Some modern poets use it occasionally, a few use it regularly, while some combine it with full rhyme. It is a useful variation of rhyme, at best a subtle device for securing a particular effect, at worst a trick. The fact is that six centuries of rhyming by English poets, without an appreciable increase in the nation's vocabulary, have stretched the resources of rhyme to what some poets consider their limit. No better indication of the limitations of English rhyme can be had than by scanning the pages of the average hymn-book. 'God', for instance, has few appropriate rhymes; 'love' and 'spirit' and 'Heaven' are in equally bad case. The earnest but not always inspired writers of hymns—and even some good poets among them—were thus obliged to use assonance: or perhaps we may say that they daringly extended the range of permissible endings. Thus 'love' can be made to pair with 'prove' or 'move'; 'spirit' with 'merit', and 'Heaven' with 'given'. Although sensitive readers are apt to feel let down by this expedient, as if the poet were lazy or incompetent, it has long been accepted as a recognized feature of hymn-writing. A poet of genius, however, makes a virtue of another's necessity. What the Victorian hymn-writer did because he had to, Wilfred Owen, the great and tragic poet of World War I, did from choice, because he saw in assonance a real extension of the means of poetry.

Consider for a minute the function of rhyme: not only does it help the memory, it satisfies an expectancy, and so gives the aesthetic fulfilment which comes from responding to a pattern.

> In Xanadu did Kubla Khan
> A stately pleasure-dome decree.

The expectation set up by 'Khan' is fulfilled doubly in 'ran'

and 'man', while in the second line the strong syllable '-ee' at the
end of 'decree' sets up a powerful demand by the inner ear for an
echo, and this is finally provided by the word 'see'. All rhyme has
this element. Blank verse must rely on other satisfactions.

Now if rhyme represents satisfaction, deliberate non-rhyme
can produce frustration. This seems to be the purpose of the
device as used by Owen.

> Let the boy try along this bayonet-blade
> How cold steel is, and keen with hunger of blood;
> Blue with all malice, like a madman's flash;
> And thinly drawn with famishing for flesh.
>
> Lend him to stroke these blind, blunt bullet-heads
> Which long to nuzzle in the hearts of lads,
> Or give him cartridges of fine zinc teeth,
> Sharp with the sharpness of grief and death.
>
> For his teeth seem for laughing round an apple.
> There lurk no claws behind his fingers supple;
> And God will grow no talons at his heels,
> Nor antlers through the thickness of his curls.

Owen burned to express his profound, almost stunned sense of
pity and indignation at the fate of the young men slaughtered on
the western front. He devised a verse appropriate to his purpose,
and of this verse he made assonance an essential element. It was
a technical triumph of great worth and power.

I undertook to say something of the heroic couplet, which may
be called the opposite of blank verse—if a poetic form can be said
to have an opposite. In blank verse no line rhymes with its neighbour. In the heroic couplet every line rhymes with its neighbour.
It consists, in fact, of a pair of rhymed iambic pentameters, and a
poem may consist of an indefinite number of such couplets.

The great age of the heroic couplet was the Restoration and
Augustan period—that is, the century from about 1660 onwards. To
trace the development of this form we must go much further back.

Chaucer wrote a good deal of poetry in the form of rhymed
iambic pentameters; but we should not apply the term 'heroic' to
his couplets. Here are some typical lines from his Franklin's Tale,
slightly modernized.

> They go and play there all the livelong day,
> And this was on the sixth morning of May,
> Which May had painted with his gentle showers
> This garden full of fresh green leaves and flowers;
> And handicraft of man so curiously
> Had laid this garden out most cunningly,
> That never was there garden of such price
> Except the garden men call Paradise.

This is a useful verse form, and has been employed by poets at most times from Chaucer to the present day. In the present century poets have tended to depart from the Chaucerian practice of ending the line at a break in the sense, and have adopted a much looser form, with the sense running on from line to line, regardless of the rhyme. Here are some lines from Rupert Brooke's *The Great Lover*, written in 1914:

> These I have loved:
>   White plates and cups, clean-gleaming,
> Ringed with blue lines; and feathery, faery dust;
> Wet roofs, beneath the lamp-light; the strong crust
> Of friendly bread; and many-tasting food;
> Rainbows; and the blue bitter smoke of wood;
> And radiant raindrops couching in cool flowers;
> And flowers themselves, that sway through sunny hours,
> Dreaming of moths that drink them under the moon;
> Then, the cool kindliness of sheets, that soon
> Smooth away trouble; and the rough male kiss
> Of blankets; grainy wood; live hair that is
> Shining and free; blue-massing clouds; the keen
> Unpassioned beauty of a great machine . . .

Brooke is here using the couplet form with great freedom. The opposite pole is represented by the Augustan 'heroic' couplet, in which each pair of lines is internally organized with extreme artifice to form a balanced whole, and the rhyme is used to clinch the meaning and hammer it home. The sense does not run on from couplet to couplet. It follows that the heroic couplet is used most appropriately in didactic or argumentative verse, where the writer has a point, or a series of points, to make, and where he pauses for assent at the end of each pair of lines. The looser, Chaucerian couplet is suited to narrative or description: the more tightly organized heroic couplet is not useful for such purposes, because a continuity in the sense, such as narrative or description demands, tends to dissolve the neatness and balance of the lines.

Dryden, writing towards the end of the seventeenth century, was the first to realize the full possibilities of the heroic couplet as a medium for didactic, satirical and polemical verse: Pope, who modelled himself on Dryden, perfected it for purposes of moralizing and abuse. Here is an example of how Dryden handled the heroic couplet. It is from his political satire, *Absalom and Achitophel*:

> The moderate sort of men, thus qualified,
> Inclined the balance to the better side;
> And David's mildness managed it so well,
> The bad found no occasion to rebel.
> But, when to sin our biased nature leans,
> The careful devil is still at hand with means;
> And providently pimps for all desires:
> The good old cause, revived, a plot requires;
> Plots, true or false, are necessary things,
> To raise up commonwealths and ruin kings.

And here is a typical passage of invective by Pope, directed against his enemy, Lady Mary Wortley Montagu, and her husband:

> Avidien, or his wife (no matter which,
> For him you'll call a dog, and her a bitch)
> Sell their presented partridges and fruits,
> And humbly live on rabbits and on roots:
> One half-pint bottle serves them both to dine,
> And is at once their vinegar and wine.
> But on some lucky day (as when they found
> A lost bank-bill, or heard their son was drowned),
> At such a feast, old vinegar to spare,
> Is what two souls so generous cannot bear:
> Oil, though it stink, they drop by drop impart,
> But souse the cabbage with a bounteous heart.

It was Pope's distinction to have exhausted the possibilities of the Augustan heroic couplet. Others used it after him. Even in the full tide of Romanticism, when the best poets had rejected the couplet and all else that smacked of the school of Pope, Byron attempted to revive it for the purpose of satire. He proved for all time that you cannot write satirical verse in this medium without sounding like an inferior imitator of Pope.

CHAPTER 18

THE LANGUAGE OF POETRY

Poetry is language. That is inescapable. It may contain ideas, but it is not ideas; it may tell a story, but it is not stories. It may express the whole range of human emotion, but unless its language is vital, fresh and surprising, those emotions will be blurred and ineffectual. Poetry, then, is vital, fresh and surprising language. Stale language will be ineffective; commonplace language will have no impact. We have discussed rhythm and rhyme, those basic devices of the poet. But without a vital language, they will be nothing. We have now to consider the nature of the language employed by poets, as if it were separable from rhythm and rhyme.

For historical reasons English is a language highly charged with poetic potentiality. This reason is to be found in the Norman conquest. At a highly critical point in England's history, she was conquered and occupied by a French-speaking people. The native language, by the year 1066, was well developed; it was a Teutonic or Germanic language, containing some, but proportionately not many, words derived from Latin, through the influence of the Church. But with the Norman conquest, those who spoke this language were governed by a people speaking a language of almost exclusively Latin origin—what scholars call a Romance language. In the course of the next few centuries these languages became inseparably blended, and in the end became modern English. The two strains—the Teutonic and the Romance —have maintained a long and harmonious alliance, but under the surface they still retain their recognizable identities. Let me quote a very simple example. When the younger Pitt died, the epitaph was engraved on his tomb, 'He died poor', which was considered a magnificent compliment for a statesman. But this epitaph was not decided upon until someone in committee had seriously suggested making it, 'He expired in necessitous circumstances'. The meaning of both sentences is the same, but the feeling is quite different. 'He expired in necessitous circumstances' contains three words derived from Latin (the Romance tongue), and conveys an impression of pompous and self-conscious grandeur; 'He died poor' consists entirely of words of Teutonic origin, and, although much more homely, has a quiet, unpretentious dignity entirely lacking in the grander version.

I don't want to suggest that the effect of Romance words in English is always pompous and pretentious. But words derived from Latin are, at any rate in the mass, more abstract, more intellectual and more logical than words of Teutonic origin. The Romance element in English thus gives an intellectual stiffening to what might otherwise be purely sensuous and down-to-earth. It is the great virtue of much of our older poetry that its language is the strong, concrete speech that uses almost entirely Teutonic words.

> The king sits in Dunfermline town
> Drinking the blude-red wine.
> 'O where will I get a skeely skipper
> To sail this new ship o' mine?'
>
> O up and spak an eldern knight,
> Sat at the king's right knee:
> 'Sir Patrick Spens is the best sailor
> That ever sailed the sea.'

It is difficult to imagine anything more graphic, simple and picturesque than this. It has an almost primitive directness and strength. There are no words in these eight lines which come directly from Latin or French. This predominantly Teutonic vocabulary is eminently suited to the ballad of *Sir Patrick Spens*, which is concerned with action and incident, not with reasoning and reflection.

As soon as poets wish to write poems of reflection and thought, they have to employ a vocabulary containing more words of Romance origin. Take the opening to one of Shakespeare's sonnets, in which he is expressing the idea that, since the hardest, most durable substances are subject to decay, frail beauty can hardly be expected to last.

> Since brass, nor stone, nor earth, nor boundless sea,
> But sad mortality o'ersways their power,
> How with this rage shall beauty hold a plea,
> Whose action is no stronger than a flower?

Here the vocabulary is predominantly Teutonic in origin, but has a stiffening of abstract Romance words which express the intellectual, rational part of the thought. 'Mortality', 'power' and 'action' carry most of the intellectual content of the lines; but the thought is saved from mere abstraction by the concrete vividness of 'brass', 'stone' and 'sea'.

Wherever Romance words preponderate, we are in danger of losing the concrete actuality of poetry in a mass of intellectual abstractions. When Milton, writing of the aim of *Paradise Lost*, says

> I may assert Eternal Providence,
> And justify the ways of God to men

we feel we are in a realm, not of graphic actuality, but of rational thought and theological argument. Even the three final Teutonic words—'ways', 'God' and 'men'—are almost as abstract as Teutonic words can be. At its best, then, English poetry, certainly from early Tudor times onwards, has maintained a balance between Teutonic and Romance elements. It might even be said that it is the test of a good poet that he has an instinct for introducing the right Romance word at the right moment. When Shakespeare makes Hamlet say, in his closing speech,

> If thou didst ever hold me in thy heart,
> Absent thee from felicity awhile,
> And in this harsh world draw thy breath in pain,
> To tell my story

we feel that the almost exaggerated Latinism of the second line adds exactly the right touch of pathetic dignity to remind us that the death of Hamlet is no ordinary death. The words subtly underline the extreme simplicity and directness of 'hold me in thy heart' and 'in this harsh world draw thy breath'.

We are reminded that poetry, like life itself, depends on a balance between the intellect and the senses, the mind and the body, thought and action. Yet in the best poetry it is the sensuous element which predominates. If there are to be ideas in a poem, it is better that they should be apprehended through concrete and sensuously realized imagery. Otherwise, we have what tends to be versified philosophy or metaphysics. Housman was right in insisting that poetry is more physical than intellectual; other poets have testified to the same belief. Consider the anonymous medieval poem in praise of the Virgin Mary.

> I sing of a maiden that is makeless,
> King of all kinges to her son she ches.[1]
> He came all so still there his mother was,
> As dew in April that falleth on the grass.
> He came all so still to his mother's bower
> As dew in April that falleth on the flower.
> He came all so still there his mother lay,
> As dew in April that falleth on the spray.
> Mother and maiden was never none but she;
> Well may such a lady God 's mother be.

This is a poem to express reverence for the purity of Mary; it is a spell intended to induce religious awe. But it does not preach, it makes no theological statement, it does not assert the purity of the Virgin Birth. By a series of three simple comparisons it suggests the idea of the Immaculate Conception and the resultant birth of the King of Kings. Because we can all visualize the freshness and purity of the morning dew on the grass, the spray and the flower, we can apprehend imaginatively the meaning of the poem without subjecting it to the intellect. It is through its direct appeal to the senses that poetry makes its lasting appeal. In responding to a good poem we seem to be, as it were, going behind thought to something more primitive and direct, taking us back to a time before conceptual thought, when language was in its infancy. It is worth taking another very different example to illustrate this important quality in poetry.

When Keats went to Scotland on a walking tour, he sent back a letter to his younger sister, Fanny, and he wrote in verse for her amusement. You may say, as Keats undoubtedly thought,

---

[1] Ches: chose.

that it is simply spontaneous doggerel, indicative of youthful high
spirits and the zest for new experience.

> There was a naughty Boy
> And a naughty Boy was he
> He ran away to Scotland
> The people for to see—
> There he found
> That the ground
> Was as hard
> That a yard
> Was as long,
> That a song
> Was as merry,
> That a cherry
> Was as red—
> That lead
> Was as weighty
> That fourscore
> Was as eighty
> That a door
> Was as wooden
> As in England—
> So he stood in
> His shoes
> And he wondered
> He wondered
> He stood in his
> Shoes and he wonder'd.

Careless doggerel this may be, but only a poet could have
written it. You will have noticed how all the senses, except that of
smell, are appealed to in these artless lines. The redness and the
sweetness of the cherry appeal to the senses of sight and taste; the
word 'song' appeals to the hearing, and the hardness of the
ground appeals to the sense of touch. We could say, then, that
the imagery in Keats's lines is concrete and the sense-impressions
they evoke are strong and vivid. It is one of the commonest ways
in which poetry engages our attention, this appeal to our senses.
A very simple definition of poetry is that it is 'felt thought'—
ideas rendered memorable by appealing to our understanding

through our senses, not simply our intellect, our bodies as well as our minds. Now the thought in Keats's lines is not very profound, nor was it meant to be. But the same sensuous strength is to be found in all Keats's best poems, and it is this, above all, which gives them their lasting attraction. It is worth pursuing this a little further. Read once more the familiar stanzas of the *Ode to Autumn*.

Season of mists and mellow fruitfulness,
   Close bosom-friend of the maturing sun;
Conspiring with him how to load and bless
   With fruit the vines that round the thatch-eaves run;
To bend with apples the moss'd cottage-trees,
   And fill all fruit with ripeness to the core;
     To swell the gourd, and plump the hazel shells
With a sweet kernel; to set budding more,
   And still more, later flowers for the bees,
   Until they think warm days will never cease,
     For Summer has o'erbrimm'd their clammy cells.

Who hath not seen thee oft amid thy store?
   Sometimes whoever seeks abroad may find
Thee sitting careless on a granary floor,
   Thy hair soft-lifted by the winnowing wind;
Or on a half-reap'd furrow sound asleep,
   Drowsed with the fume of poppies, while thy hook
     Spares the next swath and all its twinèd flowers:
And sometimes like a gleaner thou dost keep
   Steady thy laden head across a brook;
   Or by a cider-press, with patient look,
     Thou watchest the last oozings hours by hours.

Where are the songs of Spring? Ay, where are they?
   Think not of them, thou hast thy music too,—
While barrèd clouds bloom the soft-dying day,
   And touch the stubble-plains with rosy hue;
Then in a wailful choir the small gnats mourn
   Among the river sallows, borne aloft
     Or sinking as the light wind lives or dies;
And full-grown lambs loud bleat from hilly bourn;
   Hedge-crickets sing; and now with treble soft
   The redbreast whistles from a garden-croft;
     And gathering swallows twitter in the skies.

This is a poem of resignation, of reconciliation. On the surface it is a descriptive poem, and you may admit that no descriptive poetry equals it in sheer sensuous vitality. But it is more than mere description: it conveys a mood, the mood of tranquillity tinged with regret or nostalgia. It is as if Keats, foreknowing his own imminent death, were resigned to sharing in the life of nature with its seasonal cycle ending in fulfilment and death. Keats impresses on us his sense of resignation by re-creating for us the beauty of the autumn season. To do this he employs to the full his unequalled powers of sensuous evocation, so that we feel, hear, touch, taste and smell the images of autumn. The first of the three stanzas is concerned mainly with the sight, the feel and the taste of the fruit harvest; we are offered a feast for eye, hand and palate. The second stanza exploits mainly the sense of sight and the sense of smell. The corn and cider harvest is presented to us as a scene of tranquil and indolent fulfilment. In the third stanza Keats turns from this almost silent scene, warm with the languor of a September afternoon, to consider the sounds of autumn:

> Then in a wailful choir the small gnats mourn
> Among the river sallows, borne aloft
> Or sinking as the light wind lives or dies;
> And full-grown lambs loud bleat from hilly bourn;
> Hedge-crickets sing; and now with treble soft
> The redbreast whistles from a garden-croft;
> And gathering swallows twitter in the skies.

In every aspect of the autumn scene Keats achieves a sensuous realization of actuality through the clarity, vividness and abundance of his imagery.

As a young man, Gerard Manley Hopkins was a fervent admirer of Keats. It was partly through Keats's poems that he realized the appeal of the world of sense. The great decision he made was to renounce the world of sense in favour of a life of self-denial, austerity and spiritual self-perfection. This momentous act of renunciation he celebrated in *The Habit of Perfection*, in some ways his finest poem.

> Elected Silence, sing to me
> And beat upon my whorlèd ear,

Pipe me to pastures still and be
The music that I care to hear.

Shape nothing, lips; be lovely-dumb:
It is the shut, the curfew sent
From there where all surrenders come
Which only makes you eloquent.

Be shellèd, eyes, with double dark
And find the uncreated light:
This ruck and reel which you remark
Coils, keeps, and teases simple sight.

Palate, the hutch of tasty lust,
Desire not to be rinsed with wine:
The can must be so sweet, the crust
So fresh that comes in fasts divine!

Nostrils, your careless breath that spend
Upon the stir and keep of pride,
What relish shall the censers send
Along the sanctuary side!

O feel-of-primrose hands, O feet
That want the yield of plushy sward,
But you shall walk the golden street
And you unhouse and house the Lord.

And, Poverty, be thou the bride
And now the marriage feast begun,
And lily-coloured clothes provide
Your spouse not laboured-at nor spun.

Hopkins was preparing, not only to become a member of the
Roman Church, but also a priest and a Jesuit—entailing the triple
vow of poverty, chastity and obedience. That his conversion was
no simple intellectual decision but a total act of renunciation is
evidenced in the poem; he uses his marvellous command of sensuous imagery for the purpose of making his renunciation of the
life of sense. It is as if he said, 'Do not imagine that this world is
nothing to me—it is everything I have known; but it is not
enough.' The denial of the senses is, paradoxically, an even more
exquisite exercise of sensuous delight. Silence is more beautiful
than any sound, beautiful as sound can be; the 'uncreated light' of

spiritual illumination is more beautiful than the manifold and con-
fusing appearances of the world of nature; fasting is more satisfying than the lust of the palate; the smell of incense has more relish
than the casual satisfactions of the nostrils; self-denial is to give a
keener, subtler and more profound delight than all the delights of
self-indulgence. This is, in brief, the meaning of the poem: but it
is not the poem. The poem is to be apprehended, not by the intellect alone but also, and mainly, by the senses. In this way the
reader realizes, not only the nobility of Hopkins's resolution, but
also its pathos.

In this poem you will have noticed words such as 'elected',
'whorlèd', 'curfew', 'surrenders', 'eloquent', 'shellèd', 'uncreated',
'relish', 'censers', 'sanctuary', 'sward' and 'spouse'. This is in
some ways a strange choice of words. This choice is called a poet's
diction, and nothing is a clearer indication of a poet's interests and
habit of mind than his diction. From the diction of this poem you
would gather, correctly, that Hopkins was a man interested in
literature and the scriptures. The use of words like 'thou' and
'shellèd' indicates a literary turn of mind; while a number of expressions reveal a close familiarity with the Bible.

Of other poets' diction we may say that it is plain or ornate,
homely or exotic, colloquial or literary, up-to-date or archaic.
Each kind of diction has its attractions and its dangers. Excessively colloquial language degenerates into slang and vulgarity;
excessively high-flown and literary language verges on the unin-
tentionally comic.

> Say, Father Thames, for thou hast seen
>   Full many a sprightly race
> Desporting on thy margent green
>   The paths of pleasure trace,
> Who foremost now delight to cleave
> With pliant arm thy glassy wave?
>   The captive linnet which enthral?
> What idle progeny succeed
> To chase the rolling circle's speed,
>   Or urge the flying ball?

This is the third stanza of Gray's elegant *Ode on a Distant
Prospect of Eton College*, but it requires a little thought to realize

that all Gray is saying is 'Tell me, Thames, what young Etonians are now swimming in the river, catching birds, bowling hoops or playing ball on the bank?' This is a very literary diction, not without its somewhat old-world charm, but betraying the author's fear of being thought vulgar through calling a spade a spade.

For contrast here are some stanzas from Robert Graves's poem, *The Legs*, where the language is simple to the point of homeliness. No concessions are made to elegance or refinement.

> There was this road,
> And it led up-hill,
> And it led down-hill,
> And round and in and out.
>
> And the traffic was legs,
> Legs from the knees down,
> Coming and going,
> Never pausing.
>
> And the gutters gurgled
> With the rain's overflow,
> And the sticks on the pavement
> Blindly tapped and tapped.
>
> What drew the legs along
> Was the never-stopping,
> And the senseless frightening
> Fate of being legs.

Equally simple perhaps, and equally effective, is the language of W. H. Davies's *In the Country*. Here are the first three stanzas.

> This life is sweetest; in this wood
> I hear no children cry for food;
> I see no woman, white with care;
> No man, with muscles wasting here.
>
> No doubt it is a selfish thing
> To fly from human suffering;
> No doubt he is a selfish man,
> Who shuns poor creatures sad and wan.

> But 'tis a wretched life to face
> Hunger in almost every place;
> Cursed with a hand that's empty, when
> The heart is full to help all men.

It is obvious that the strength and simplicity of Davies's feelings are better conveyed by plain and simple words than by anything ornate or literary. That such a diction is suited not only to country subjects but also to industrial scenes is shown by these lines from a contemporary poet, Charles Madge, who is clearly fascinated by the imagery of a technical age.

> With an effort Grant swung the great block,
> The swivel operated and five or six men
> Crouched under the lee of the straight rock.
>
> They waited in silence or counting ten,
> They thrust their fingers in their wet hair,
> The steel sweated in their hands. And then
>
> The clouds hurried across a sky quite bare,
> The sounds of the station, three miles off, ceased,
> The dusty birds hopped keeping watch.

Like Gray, Milton was what we should call a literary poet. He was immensely learned, and his wide reading gave him an immense vocabulary, a vocabulary drawn from the printed page rather than from the common speech of ordinary men and women. You are aware of this at almost any point in his poems; you are aware, too, of a man extremely conscious of his dignity as a poet. Here are some lines from *Paradise Regained*.

> They err who count it glorious to subdue
> By conquest far and wide, to overrun
> Large countries, and in field great battles win,
> Great cities by assault. What do these worthies
> But rob and spoil, burn, slaughter, and enslave
> Peaceable nations, neighbouring or remote,
> Made captive, yet deserving freedom more
> Than those their conquerors, who leave behind
> Nothing but ruin wheresoe'er they rove,
> And all the flourishing works of peace destroy;

> Then swell with pride, and must be titled Gods,
> Great Benefactors of mankind, Deliverers,
> Worshipped with temple, priest, and sacrifice?

'They err who count it glorious to subdue' seems to be a somewhat laboured, yet highly dignified way of saying, 'You are wrong if you think it glorious to conquer', and this lofty, indirect utterance does not belong only to the poetry of past ages. Here are some lines from a living American, John Crowe Ransom. In *Dead Boy* he describes and comments on the reactions of a Virginian community to the death of the late-born son of an old family, and the shock to their pride.

> The elder men have strode by the box of death
> To the wide flag porch, and muttering low send round
> The bruit of the day. O friendly waste of breath!
> Their hearts are hurt with a deep dynastic wound.
>
> He was pale and little, the foolish neighbours say;
> The first-fruits, saith the preacher, the Lord hath taken;
> But this was the old tree's late branch wrenched away,
> Aggrieving the sapless limbs, the shorn and shaken.

Among the chief resources of poetry are the devices we call metaphor and simile. Simile is the simpler to perceive and to understand; metaphor is the more compressed and suggestive. If you wish to explain to someone what something looks like which he has not seen before, you may do this by comparing it to something else. If you wish to extend the resources of language, you can do this by inventing metaphors. It is probable that in the earliest stages in the development of our language, this was the means by which much of the language itself was created. Our ancestors had something like our word 'stone' to denote the hard, mineral object we all know. When they wanted to convey the idea of someone or something remaining perfectly motionless, they coined the word 'to stand', which is connected with 'stone'. Originally, then, the verb 'to stand' (which to us is not metaphorical at all) meant 'to behave like a stone'—that is, 'to keep still'. Thus metaphor—seeing one thing in terms of another—is at the root of language, and poetry extends its range by the use of metaphor; metaphor itself is a sort of compressed simile. If you think of the idea of 'time', it is very difficult to convey it to any-one else. All we know is that it 'flows' or progresses from one moment to the next, one year to another. If we say that time flows, we imply that it moves in a fixed course, like a river. In the word 'flow' we imply a comparison with a river.

> Time like an ever-rolling stream
> Bears all its sons away;
> They fly forgotten as a dream
> Dies at the opening day.

So Isaac Watts, paraphrasing the Psalmist, describes the fleet-ing nature of human life, as distinct from the eternity of God. He uses two similes, one to suggest the relentless passage of time, the other to suggest the impermanence of human life. When Shake-speare, in *Macbeth*, wanted to give a brief, vivid impression of the atmosphere of treachery and suspicion that existed in Scotland during the dictatorship of the usurper, he said, 'There's daggers in men's smiles'. He might have said, 'Beneath an appearance of cordiality men conceal treacherous intentions, as if they were con-cealing daggers beneath innocent-looking cloaks'. This is the full meaning of his words. But how much more compressed and graphic is the simple five-word sentence, 'There's daggers in men's smiles'.

Shakespeare used metaphor and simile instinctively. It is im-possible to imagine his having consciously worked out the elabor-ate texture of metaphor which makes the language of his plays so striking and memorable. Other poets of his time used such devices more consciously. Here is a stanza from Ben Jonson's *The Triumph of Charis*, in which a series of comparisons is used to bring home to the reader the beauty of the lady he is celebrating.

> Have you seen but a bright lily grow
> Before rude hands have touched it?
> Have you marked but the fall of the snow
> Before the soil hath smutched it?
> Have you felt the wool of beaver,
> Or swan's down ever?
> Or have smelt o' the bud o' the brier
> Or the nard in the fire?

> Or have tasted the bag of the bee?
> O so white, O so soft, O so sweet is she!

In later times we have to go to Keats for language of such rich and sensuous suggestion as this.

Metaphor and simile are among the means by which poets who feel that language has become stale can renew its force and vitality. Early in the twentieth century an English poet, T. E. Hulme, was concerned at finding the language of poetry degenerated into something woolly and imprecise. He wrote few poems, but all were brief and clear-cut. He was determined that not a word should be superfluous, and that each image should compel the reader to make a visual and intellectual effort at comprehension. Here is one of his poems, *The Embankment* (*The fantasia of a fallen gentleman on a cold, bitter night*).

> Once, in finesse of fiddles, found I ecstasy,
> In a flash of gold heels on the hard pavement.
> Now see I
> That warmth's the very stuff of poesy.
> Oh, God, make small
> The old star-eaten blanket of the sky,
> That I may fold it round me and in comfort lie.

In the brilliant metaphor of 'the old star-eaten blanket of the sky', he is perhaps unconsciously echoing Shakespeare's 'the blanket of the dark' in *Macbeth*. In another of his brief poems, *Conversion*, he makes striking use of simile:

> Light-hearted I walked into the valley wood
> In the time of hyacinths,
> Till beauty like a scented cloth
> Cast over, stifled me. I was bound
> Motionless and faint of breath
> By loveliness that is her own eunuch.
>
> Now pass I to the final river
> Ignominiously, in a sack, without sound,
> As any peeping Turk to the Bosphorus.

In yet another poem Hulme wishes to convey the contrast between the harvest moon and the stars. He accordingly uses two very original similes. This is called *Autumn*.

A touch of cold in the Autumn night—
I walked abroad,
And saw the ruddy moon lean over a hedge
Like a red-faced farmer.
I did not stop to speak, but nodded,
And round about were the wistful stars
With white faces like town children.

A modern American poet, Hart Crane, tried also to make his readers see things in a light they had never appeared in before. In *North Labrador* you find him using a subtle and complex web of metaphor and simile to describe an unfamiliar landscape. He relies on no well-worn comparisons; everything is new, as if seen for the first time. We need to concentrate as closely as possible, the mind's eye fully attentive. If we allow our attention to wander for a moment, the picture goes out of focus.

A land of leaning ice
Hugged by plaster-grey arches of sky,
Flings itself silently
Into eternity.

'Has no one come here to win you,
Or left you with the faintest blush
Upon your glittering breasts?
Have you no memories, O Darkly Bright?'

Cold-hushed, there is only the shifting of moments
That journey toward no Spring—
No birth, no death, no time nor sun
In answer.

I have dwelt at some length on the diction and imagery of poetry, though I could go on almost indefinitely. Two things are apparent: the first is that the resources of poetry are as inexhaustible as human experience itself. Provided there is an audience for poetry, however small, and provided we are not dead to new experience, there is a future for poetry. The second thing is that, without freshness and originality of language, no poet can achieve lasting success. However sincere he may be, however open to emotional experience, however much he longs to infect others with the excitement that this experience has given him, he

M

is powerless without a command of English. That is why, in making an assessment of a new poem, or the work of a poet you have not come across before, you must look, not only at what he says, but, first of all, at the way in which he says it. In the end the two things are one. The apparatus of modern life, with its multiplicity of formal documents and newspaper reports, accustoms us to language that is dead and stale. If it is merely a guide to action, it cannot be helped. But all this deadening paper threatens to wrap us in a covering of unreality, and this in turn leads to routine and boredom. By contrast, poetry stands for life and freshness, vitality and newness of experience. Poetry is the enemy of official jargon and stale, boring expression.

CHAPTER 19

CONCLUSION

In these pages I have introduced you to poetry. If you had, as I expect you had, an interest in it already, I hope that interest has been increased by reading these pages. I have said something of the nature of poetry and of the men and women who write it; I have said a little about its long history, and how its character has slowly changed through the centuries. I have outlined the technique or craft of poetry, and I have tried to show, by many examples, the kind of poem I think most worth reading and knowing. The question of whether poetry is worth while, and whether you can or can't do without it, can only be left to you. I write as one who has loved it since the days of my first nursery rhyme and as one who has tried to write it almost since I learned to write. You may do without poetry: most people do—to their cost, in my opinion. There are many demands on your time— sport, social life, music and the other arts—quite apart from the business of what Wordsworth called 'getting and spending'.

There are some who believe that poetry has now become so specialized that it is the concern only of other specialists—those who write poems and those who make it their trade to criticize it or teach literature in schools and colleges. I don't deny that in some respects the field of poetry has narrowed since those days, many centuries ago, when the majority could neither read nor write. As prose literature has developed, the need for poetry in several fields has declined: especially the fields of drama and fiction. Yet this very narrowing of the poetic field has meant a more intensive cultivation. We now no longer demand narrative or dramatic poetry, but in one important respect we still need what is not very happily called lyric poetry. The great aim of this is, as I have shown, to express emotion, to convey a view of life which includes, not only rational thought, but also feeling. It is conceivable that we may one day achieve a kind of mass civilization in which personal feelings are a prohibited luxury, and all that is required of us as thinking and feeling creatures is the mass response of a collectivized insect colony. That time has not yet come. We are still thinking and feeling individuals, despite all the pressures to become ants. Poetry exists to nourish and strengthen our individuality. This is not to say that there is no room for poetry of a more social character, especially popular song: there is said to be a folk-song revival, though as yet this seems to me self-conscious and uncertain of its direction. You may think and feel as others do: the less enlightened sections of the press, the radio and the television would like you to do so exclusively. But if you think and feel as an individual, with your own personal response to experience, your own private problems and psychological stresses, poetry has something to give you.

Poets are the pioneers and explorers in the world of feeling. Wherever you find yourself in that world, a poet may have been there before you. He will not have had your precise emotions nor experienced exactly your problem; but his experience will have had enough in common with yours for you to feel supported and reassured by what he has written. If poetry now seems too specialized for the ordinary reader, this is the greatest possible misfortune. For potentially it is the least specialized activity of the human spirit. We all use language. When a poet writes

> Alone, alone, all, all alone,
> Alone on a wide, wide sea!

or

> Love still has something of the Sea,
> From whence his Mother rose;

or

> Exultation is the going
> Of an inland soul to sea,

he is putting into words a fact of experience which you also know, or to which you have access. When you come to read contemporary poetry, you may not find it so simple: but it is worth the effort to understand, and only familiarity can bring understanding. If I had to answer in a single sentence the question, 'Why should I read poetry?' I would say, 'Because it is the surest way in which to get to know yourself.'

There is perhaps one surer way—that is, to *write* poems. Far more people—especially but by no means exclusively when young—write poems than is commonly supposed. This is because they feel the need to express their feelings or to understand some psychological problem by which they are confronted. If more people wrote poems, there would be less need for the solution of psychological difficulties by analytical methods. I don't mean that poems are written simply because people want to 'get something out of their system'; but this need is at least an element in poetic creation. If I say that anyone to whom language is a reality is a potential poet, I don't mean that he is necessarily a potentially good poet. This would be too much to hope. The fact that good poems have at all times been rare, however, does not mean that it is a bad thing for much poetry to be written that never gets into print. The more run-of-the-mill poets there are in any age, the better the good poets tend to be. The Elizabethan age is scarcely more remarkable for its few great poets—Shakespeare, Spenser, Marlowe and the rest—than for its dozens of lesser men who could write at least a passable sonnet or song because poetry was then 'in the air'. When I say that anybody may be a potential poet, I don't mean that I believe in the emergence of another Shakespeare or Blake at any particular time: I do mean, however, that since there was no ascertainable reason why either of these men should have been a great poet, there is also no reason why any other individual should not be a poet. I see a good deal of unpublished poetry, most of it not very good: what matters, however, is that it should be written, and that a lot of people think it worth while to write it, even without any clear hope of fame or profit. The continued existence, despite every discouragement, of this amateur poetic activity, as I may call it, makes me increasingly sure of one thing. I am very suspicious of any definition of a poet which makes him appear as a person of unusual experience or excessive sensibility. The emotions of a poet and the poet's sensibility are not exclusive to the poet: if they were, they would be of little interest to others. We know much of

Keats's passion for beauty, of Shelley's desire for freedom, of Hardy's nostalgia for past joy, of Clare's delight in nature, of Hopkins's religious ardour, of the conflict of intellect and passion in Donne: but these things may exist, to a greater or lesser degree of intensity, in all of us. All we can say for certain about these men, as distinct from the rest of mankind, is that their inner lives were more readily expressible in striking and memorable language than is the case with most others. We may say, if we choose, not that a poet is subject to greater psychological stresses than others, but that he is more continuously and intensely impelled to relieve or resolve these tensions through the medium of language. Yet even that may not be quite true: Who is to say that the writing of poems was more compulsive upon Keats or Shakespeare than upon the most incompetent and unsuccessful burner of midnight oil? It may be true, but it is not very helpful, simply to say that Keats was inspired, and the nocturnal scribbler is not. I think we can get a little nearer the truth than this.

A good poet is, as a rule, someone who has made and who makes a continuous study of poetry, not only as a writer but as a reader. There are of course exceptions. But on the whole we can be fairly confident that the true poet has not only read a good deal of poetry but, more important, has read at least some poetry with insight and passion. This alone will not make a poet, any more than continual study, effort and desire will make an ordinary violinist into a Menuhin. Many other qualities are needed. Fate is notoriously unfair and capricious. In the world of poetry and the arts it is not always the industrious and deserving who get to the top of the class. Fortunately, however, it is not important to get to the top of the class. To be a poet of merit or distinction is a matter of destiny, outside human control: those whom this fate has befallen have not always been made happy by it. Some indeed have regarded it as a curse. It has been their fate, not so much to achieve consciously some eminence or distinction, as to be the mouthpiece of the thoughts and feelings of their fellows.

To be a poet, then, is more an unsought responsibility than a coveted distinction. Good poems are written because they have to be, not because their authors want them to be. Yet more people feel the urge to express themselves than have the confidence to do so. What matters is that all who feel impelled to write poems should do so, without concerning themselves with success or failure. In this way they can achieve a sense of community with those pioneers of feeling whose work they have enjoyed and are grateful for. If they do not feel impelled to write poems, but only to read and know and understand the poetry of others, so much the better for them. The English language certainly has yielded enough poetry to give any normal reader a lifetime of new experience and imaginative revelation.

Index of Poems Quoted

in full or in part

General Index